Pakistan's Civil Society: Alternative Channels to Countering Violent Extremism

Dr. Hedieh Mirahmadi, Mehreen Farooq and Waleed Ziad

OCTOBER 2012

WORDE
World Organization for Resource Development and Education
1875 I Street, NW, Suite 500
Washington DC, 20006
Tel: 1-202-595-1355
Fax: 1-202-318-2582
Email: staff@worde.org
Web: www.worde.org

© Copyright 2012 by World Organization for Resource Development and Education

Printed and bound in the United States of America. All rights reserved. No part of this book may be reproduced in any form or by any electronic or mechanical means, including information storage and retrieval systems, without permission in writing from the publisher, WORDE.

Front Cover Photos by Mehreen Farooq.

Captions (clockwise): Civil society activists in Swat discussing strategies for promoting pluralism; young boys studying in a madrassa in southern Punjab, a region in which traditional Muslim groups are working to deter at-risk youth from joining militant groups; and young girls playing at the shrine of the revered poet-saint, Saidu Baba, which was attacked by the Taliban in 2009.

Published and Distributed by:

World Organization for Resource Development and Education (WORDE)
1875 I Street NW, Suite 500
Washington, DC 20006
Tel: (202) 595-1355
Fax: (202) 318-2582
Email: staff@worde.org
Web: www.worde.org

First Edition: October 2012
Pakistan's Civil Society: Alternative Channels to Countering Violent Extremism

PRINTED IN THE UNITED STATES OF AMERICA

ABOUT WORDE

The World Organization for Resource Development and Education (WORDE) is a nonprofit, educational organization whose mission is to enhance communication and understanding between Muslim and non-Muslim communities, and to strengthen moderate Muslim institutions worldwide to mitigate social and political conflict.

WORDE shapes public policy by cultivating a better understanding of Islamic ideologies that promote pluralism and service to humanity – while exposing the roots of extremism that disrupt the peaceful coexistence of societies everywhere. Our specialists are academics, theologians, development experts, and policy analysts who develop effective, long-term solutions in the key areas of educational reform, resource development, and international security. Many of them serve as advisors to various US government agencies as well as international organizations and governments.

Across the world, in Pakistan, Afghanistan, Indonesia, Singapore, and the United Kingdom, WORDE is actively engaged with traditional Muslim networks to strengthen their communities against the rising threat of violent extremism. We believe the US government and nonprofit sector should establish a good working relationship with religious and cultural leaders who adamantly reject the radical ideologies of terrorists and could serve as a bulwark against militants. Our strategy includes investing in human capital, facilitating linkages with local and international public policymakers, and establishing international networks of moderate Muslim scholars, cultural groups, and thought leaders that empower one another to generate positive change.

ACKNOWLEDGEMENTS

We would like to thank Qamar-ul Huda at the United States Institute of Peace, Shuja Nawaz at the Atlantic Council, Peter Bergen at the New America Foundation and Dr. Akbar S. Ahmed, the Ibn Khaldun Chair of Islamic Studies at the American University for their comments and support of this project. In addition we are thankful to Shamoun Idrees Maayr, Javed Jabbar, Zahra Hussain, Shaykh Usman Cheepa, Imam Irfan Chisti and Imam Shahid Mursaleen for their assistance in facilitating our research in Pakistan. We are particularly grateful for the research assistance provided by Sairah Zaidi, Mariam Saadi, and Maryyum Usmani. We would also like to express our appreciation for the support we received from the Pakistani American community who encouraged us to pursue this project. Finally we would like to thank Muhammad Khaliq Khan for his service and assistance in Pakistan.

TABLE OF CONTENTS

Executive Summary	5
Introduction	7
The Rise of Extremist Groups in Pakistan	16
Government-Led Counter Extremism Efforts	20
Civil Society Level Efforts to Counter Extremism	23
Limitations & Challenges	34
Recommendations	36
Conclusion	41

EXECUTIVE SUMMARY

Terrorist attacks, internal conflicts fueled by ethnic and sectarian violence, and a myriad of governance and development challenges constrain the Government of Pakistan's ability to counter violent extremism effectively. Though the US continues its pressure on political and military officials in Pakistan to take stronger measures in eradicating militant groups in the region, its leaders have failed to adopt a systematic approach to empower Pakistan's civil society as a bulwark against violent extremism.

Despite the potential of moderate networks to promote peace and conflict resolution, Pakistan's civil society has been largely understudied. The purpose of this report is to examine the breadth and scope of Pakistan's civil society, and its capacity for peace-building and countering violent extremism (CVE) initiatives. Its findings are the result of a year-long study featuring twelve weeks of field work in which WORDE researchers travelled to over 35 cities and villages at risk of violent extremism—from Peshawar, Swat, and the Federally Administered Tribal Areas (FATA), to Azad Jammu and Kashmir (AJK), southern Punjab, interior Sindh and Karachi to meet with over 100 civil society networks. (See map below.)

This report begins by exploring the rise of extremist groups in Pakistan and the avenues through which they increase their influence in society. The next section discusses government-led initiatives to counter extremism. This is followed by a broad overview of the scope and capacity of Pakistan's civil society. Efforts to build public awareness and counter violent extremism are discussed along with challenges and limitations. The final section of the report provides recommendations for US policymakers on the potential of building the capacity of Pakistan's civil society to improve the efficacy of existing initiatives and encourage the creation of new projects.

Although faith-based organizations (traditional Muslim networks[1]) and non-faith based organizations (culturally Muslim networks[2]) are engaged in a variety of peace-building initiatives, our analysis focuses largely on traditional Muslim networks, which have been largely understudied.

There are several overarching factors that explain the significance of traditional Muslim networks. Throughout the country, and particularly in conflict areas, traditional Muslim networks are building and expanding moderate madrasas to counter the proliferation of radical ideologies offered by violent extremists. These moderate madrasas often serve as "hubs," coordinating resources and projects among their satellite schools, affiliated social welfare institutions and media outlets. Because these networks are active on every level of society, they are critical channels for disseminating anti-extremist messages within a conservative religious framework that is palatable to at-risk individuals as well as the broader population.

For the past three decades extremists have undermined moderate networks through various means. Militant factions use brutal intimidation tactics to coerce populations to support their movements and in much of the tribal areas bordering Afghanistan, moderate religious and political leaders are assassinated for speaking out against the Taliban. Extremist groups have also expanded their influence at the institutional level by waging a fierce battle over the ownership of existing religious institutions which

---

[1] "Traditional Muslim Networks" include of Sunni and Shi'a faith-based organizations that promote peace and social cohesion, and unconditionally reject terrorism, suicide bombings, and other Taliban ideologies.

[2] "Culturally Muslim" refers to groups who identify with being Muslim, however their mission and organizational focus may not necessarily be religious or faith-based. Often secular in character and mandate, these organizations have shared values and policies with the US such as supporting human rights, gender equality, freedom of worship, respect and tolerance of diversity, and a rejection of violent extremism.

have historically rejected terrorism. Finally, militants also capitalize on socio-political grievances to gain support.

To address the threat of extremism, the Government of Pakistan has implemented several policies – from madrasa reforms to organizing de-radicalization camps - however the efficacy of these programs has been mixed. In place of a comprehensive government-led strategy to counter extremism, Pakistan's civil society is faced with the responsibility to fill in the gaps.

Our study has determined that faith-based and non-faith based civil society organizations (CSOs) are promoting collective action to counter extremism through multiple channels. Public rallies, demonstrations, and conferences are convened by civil society leaders to create strategies and slogans for anti-terror campaigns as well as to mobilize various segments of the population. CSOs are also using newspapers, television and radio programs to generate public awareness about the causes of extremism. Art is increasingly being used for contemporary, young audiences as well.

CSOs have also organized several CVE initiatives. By improving access to education, and facilitating inter-faith and inter-ethnic dialogues, moderate educators are challenging the intolerant ideologies propagated by extremists. Religious scholars are also using fatwas, public lectures and debates to denounce terrorism at the theological level within a conservative religious framework.

While the initiatives highlighted in this report provide valuable models for countering extremism, they should be improved and replicated on a larger scale to create a sustained national movement. Civil society leaders cite several challenges that prevent them from harnessing their potential such as a lack of security, government support, and funding. Many activists are also finding it increasingly difficult to publically address sensitive issues in the current socio-political environment. To address this challenge, relevant government-funded programs from the United States Institute of Peace to the United State Commission on International Religious Freedom should work with civil society leaders to develop projects that promote religious freedom and inter-ethnic social harmony.

Moderate networks also cite a lack of consensus-building skills to create coalitions and partnerships. The US Embassy in Islamabad should create venues and networking opportunities for faith-based and non-faith-based groups to develop a coherent national counter-extremism strategy.

Good governance and leadership development, conflict resolution and coalition building, communications and media training are additional areas in which material support and expertise are needed to build moderate networks' institutional capacity. Relevant US Government agencies from the State Department, US Agency for International Development, and the US Institute of Peace should invest in training initiatives. The US Government could also facilitate opportunities for the diaspora community to partner with Pakistan-based CSOs to provide the requisite skills training.

Despite widespread criticism of US foreign policy in Pakistan, civil society leaders – both faith-based and secular - expressed a willingness to engage with the US on these issues. Ultimately, a strategic partnership with Pakistan's civil society can both rebuild trust at this critical juncture, and usher in a new chapter in US-Pakistan relations.

INTRODUCTION

After more than a decade of cooperation in the war against violent extremist networks, several incidents in the past two years have severely strained US-Pakistan relations. In Washington, policymakers from Capitol Hill to the Pentagon have questioned Pakistan's commitment to eradicating extremism.[3] Some suggest that Pakistan is providing tacit support and safe havens to militant groups, and have moved to suspend US foreign assistance to Pakistan.[4] In response, officials in Islamabad assert that the US has violated Pakistan's sovereignty on a number of occasions, from continuing drone strikes to the unilateral operation on the bin Laden compound.[5] When US-led NATO forces launched a cross-border attack, unintentionally killing 24 Pakistani soldiers last November, Pakistan responded by closing off NATO supply routes to Afghanistan – bringing relations to an all-time low. While prospects for improving U.S.-Pakistan relations at the track I level are diminishing, there is a great potential to explore alternative channels at the civil society level.[6]

A NEW DIRECTION FOR US-PAKISTAN RELATIONS

The prevalence of violent extremism in Pakistan, the sixth largest country in the world in terms of population, underscores the need for a paradigm shift in US- Pakistan relations. In the past two years, hundreds of people have died in Pakistan as a result of sectarian violence;[7] and nearly a dozen major Sufi shrines have been attacked.[8] Communal conflict has also resurfaced. In March 2011, the Tehreek-i-Taliban Pakistan claimed responsibility for killing Pakistan's only Christian federal minister, Mr. Shahbaz Bhatti, the Minister of Minority Affairs.[9] In addition, inter-ethnic and inter-tribal conflicts have destabilized regions of the country from Quetta to Karachi.

Although the US has periodically sought to empower Pakistan's civil society as a bulwark against extremism, a systematic long-term approach has not yet been adopted. As a result, the majority of US-Pakistan relations have been conducted on a government-to-government or a military-to-military level. This dynamic is reflected in how the $20 billion aid package to Pakistan has been allocated.[10] From 2002-2008, approximately 75% of foreign assistance to Pakistan was explicitly for military and security

---

[3] Associated Press, "Panetta: Patience with Pakistan 'Reaching Limits,'" *NPR*, June 7, 2012 http://www.npr.org/2012/06/07/154480171/panetta-visits-afghanistan-as-violence-spikes

[4] In May, 2011 Congressman Dana Rohrabacher introduced the "Defund the United States Assistance to Pakistan Act of 2011" bill and in July, 2011 President Obama suspended and cancelled millions of dollars of aid to the Pakistani military.
Eric Schmitt and Jane Perlez, "US Is Deferring Millions in Pakistani Military Aid," *New York Times*, July 9, 2011 http://www.nytimes.com/2011/07/10/world/asia/10intel.html?pagewanted=all

[5] Jon Boone, "Pakistani MPs say US Drone Strikes Must End Before Relations Improve," *The Guardian*, March 20, 2012, http://www.guardian.co.uk/world/2012/mar/20/pakistani-us-drone-strikes-relations

[6] Shams Momand, "Pakistan Stops NATO supplies after Deadly Raid," *Reuters*, November 26, 2011, http://www.reuters.com/article/2011/11/26/us-pakistan-nato-idUSTRE7AP03S20111126

[7] http://www.satp.org/satporgtp/countries/pakistan/database/sect-killing.htm

[8] "Attacks on Sufi Shrines in Pakistan," *CIRCLe*, http://www.terrorismwatch.com.pk/Attacks%20on%20Shrines%20In%20Pakistan.html

[9] Zohra Yusuf, "Declared Profane," *Dawn*, December 31, 2011, http://dawn.com/2011/12/31/human-rights-2011-declared-profane/

[10] Susan Cornwell, "Factbox: US has Allocated $20 billion for Pakistan," *Reuters*, April 21, 2011, http://www.reuters.com/article/2011/04/21/us-pakistan-usa-aid-factbox-idUSTRE73K7F420110421

purposes, with only 10% allocated for development.[11] Although the 2008 Kerry-Lugar-Bergman bill marked a shift in this approach by raising the amount of civilian aid over a four-year period, without a sustainable strategy to engage Pakistan's civil society, both the US and Pakistan have been unable to make substantial progress in countering extremism.

There is an immense potential to rebuild US-Pakistan relations at the civil society level by addressing issues of mutual concern such as terrorism. According to the Pakistani government, since September 11, 2001 terrorism has claimed approximately 35,000 Pakistani lives.[12] Civil society leaders across Pakistan acknowledge the toll terrorism has taken on their communities, and public opinion polls indicate that Al-Qaeda is still widely unpopular among Pakistanis.[13]

Faced with increasing threats and inadequate public institutions, communities across Pakistan have had to devise their own innovative strategies to counter extremism.[14] These bottom-up strategies, discussed in greater detail in this report, are tailored to reflect regional customs and sensitivities. They are also perceived to have greater legitimacy and credibility than initiatives implemented by international organizations.

Given the effectiveness of local efforts, the next chapter of US-Pakistan relations should begin by engaging and empowering Pakistan's civil society to improve the efficacy and impact of their existing programs in addition to developing new initiatives. Failing to capitalize on civil society resources would represent a significant missed opportunity for revitalizing U.S.-Pakistan relations at this critical juncture in the global war against terrorism.

This report will begin by discussing our research methodology. The next section will explore the rise of extremist groups in Pakistan and the avenues through which they increase their influence in society. The following section will briefly discuss government-led initiatives to counter extremism. This is followed by a broad overview of the scope and capacity of Pakistan's civil society to promote peace. Regional and national efforts to build public awareness and counter violent extremism are discussed along with their challenges and limitations. The final section of the report provides recommendations for US policymakers to build the capacity of Pakistan's civil society and improve the effectiveness of existing initiatives, in addition to facilitating new projects.

---

[11] S. Akbar Zaidi, "Who Benefits from US Aid to Pakistan?" *Carnegie Endowment for International Peace*, Policy Outlook: September 21, 2011, http://carnegieendowment.org/files/pakistan_aid2011.pdf
[12] "With 35,000 Deaths, and $68 Billion in Losses, Pakistan Fights On," *The News*, September 12, 2011, http://www.thenews.com.pk/Todays-News-13-8732-With-35000-deaths-and-$68-bn-in-losses-Pakistan-fights-on
[13] "On Anniversary of bin Laden's Death, Little Backing of Al Qaeda," *Pew Research Center*, April 30, 2012. http://www.pewglobal.org/2012/04/30/on-anniversary-of-bin-ladens-death-little-backing-of-al-qaeda/
[14] Huma Yusuf, "An Inadequate Response," *Dawn*, April 23, 2012, http://dawn.com/2012/04/23/an-inadequate-response/

THE SIZE AND SCOPE OF PAKISTAN'S CIVIL SOCIETY

Despite its potential to promote peace and denounce radical narratives, Pakistan's civil society has been largely understudied.[15] It is estimated that there are approximately 100,000 NGOs operating in Pakistan.[16] However, the exact numbers of NGOs in Pakistan are unknown because nearly half of Pakistan's civil society organizations are unregistered and official registration records are not routinely updated. Given the large proportion of unregistered organizations, this report uses the term Civil Society Organizations (CSOs). CSOs refers to registered and unregistered organizations (that do not operate within the apparatus of the government), such as coalitions, trade unions, labor unions, professional associations, faith-based organizations, cultural associations, community based organizations, social welfare organizations, not-for-profit health providers, non-for-profit schools, philanthropic foundations, and voluntary organizations.

Previous research suggests that the number of CSOs in Pakistan has grown substantially since the 1980s due to a number of factors.[17] The liberalization of Pakistan's media has played a critical role in increasing public awareness about extremism and other national security threats. The expansion of information available has increased a desire among youth to become more involved in their communities. According to several civil society leaders that we interviewed, youth have joined the non-profit sector at an unprecedented rate because they lack confidence in the government to address social issues. As a result, there has been a growth of youth-led CSOs in the past five years. Increased mobile and internet connectivity has also enabled organizations to collaborate their resources more effectively. Social media platforms such as Facebook and Twitter have also created a space to address a wide range of social welfare issues.

Given the recent push by social activists to create new organizations, the question is not whether these religious and civil institutions will continue to play a role, but rather how the US can invest and integrate them into peace-building initiatives.

OUR METHODOLOGY

This report is the result of a year-long study in which WORDE researchers travelled to regions at-risk of violent extremism (see map on page 10). During the course of the fieldwork, the team established relationships with local civil society leaders in each region who facilitated meetings with their partners and other actors within their networks. This research methodology, known as "respondent driven sampling," enabled the team to identify groups such as rural community based organizations or faith-based organizations that have been traditionally understudied.

---

[15] Critical statistics about the size and scope of Pakistan's civil society are based on reports compiled over ten years ago. See for example, Dr. Aisha Ghaus-Pasha, Haroon Jamal, and Muhammad Asif Iqbal, "Dimensions of the Nonprofit Sector in Pakistan (Preliminary Estimates), *Social Policy and Development Centre,* 2002;
Adnan Sattar Rabia Baig, "Civil Society in Pakistan: A Preliminary Report on the CIVICUS index on Civil Society Project in Pakistan," *NGO Resource Center,* August 2001.
[16] Khawar Ghumman, "Over 100,000 NGOs Operate in Pakistan: Minister," *Dawn.com,* June 29, 2009.
[17] Nadia Naviwala, "Harnessing Local Capacity: U.S. Assistance and NGOs in Pakistan," *Harvard Kennedy School Policy Analysis Exercise*, Spring 2010.

Our team interviewed civil society leaders in over 35 cities and villages, from Peshawar, Swat, and the Federally Administered Tribal Areas (FATA), to Azad Jammu and Kashmir (AJK), southern Punjab, interior Sindh, and Karachi. The team met with over 100 civil society organizations which were selected based on their potential to a) promote peace and social cohesion, b) counter radical ideologies within a cultural or religious paradigm, or c) conduct humanitarian assistance in conflict-affected regions. These organizations and their initiatives are discussed in this report; however the names of several community leaders and organizations have been omitted to protect their privacy and to ensure their security.

Map of Fieldwork

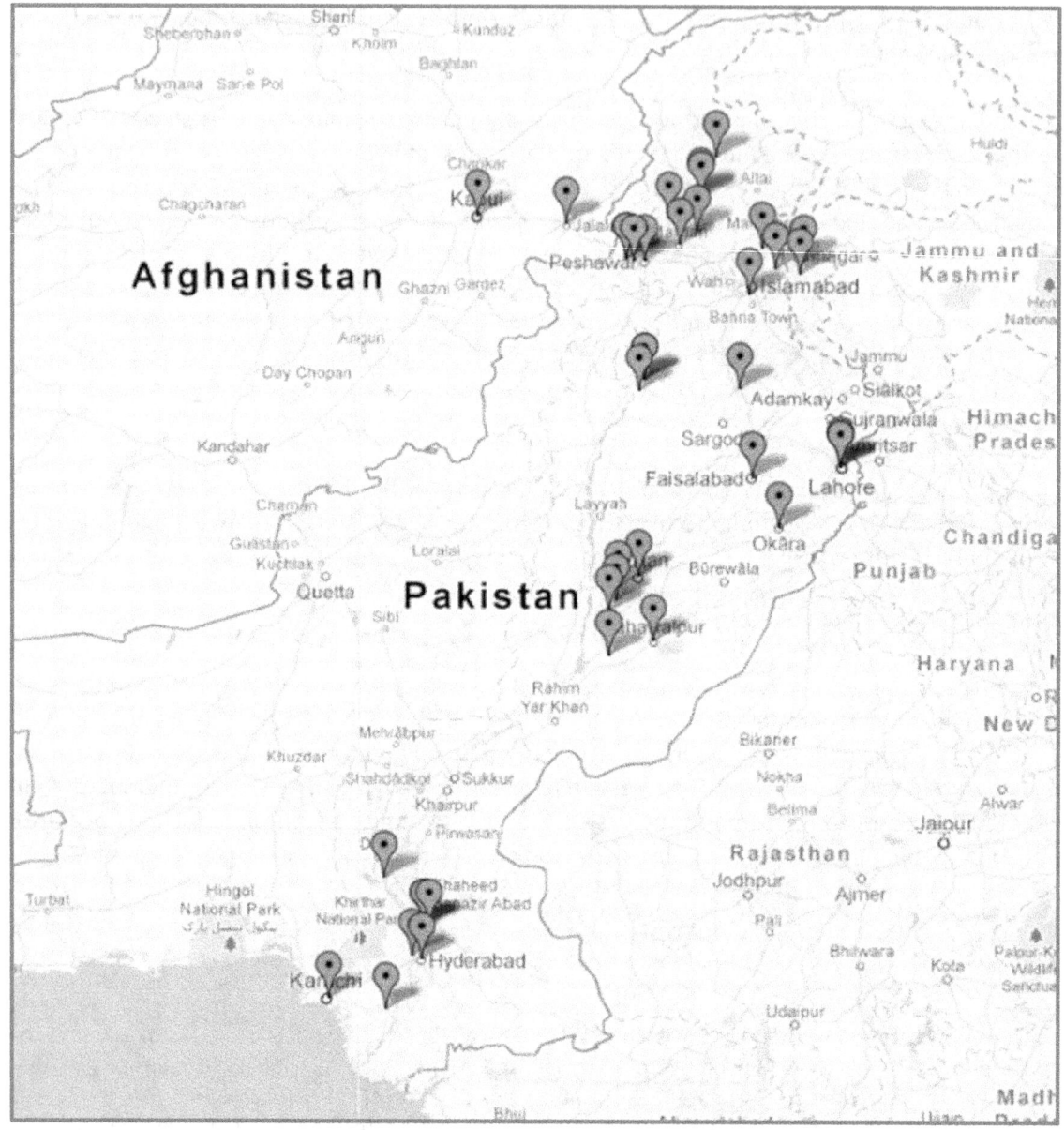

Source: Google Maps

Selection of Population Sample

Interviews were focused on three key groups playing a central role in efforts to counter violent extremism (CVE):

1. Educators and peace activists that are promoting peace, social cohesion, non-violent conflict resolution, and interethnic and interfaith dialogue;
2. Scholars and community activists who have the capacity to counter radical narratives within an authentic, cultural or religious paradigm; and
3. Faith-based and non-faith-based social welfare organizations that are administering post-crisis humanitarian aid and development assistance in conflict-affected areas.

Impact of Findings

Our study has identified over one hundred civil society networks throughout Pakistan that engage in peace-building initiatives. Networks can consist of dozens of sub-organizations (e.g. schools, political parties, publishing houses, orphanages, charitable foundations, and television or radio stations). Major madrasas, for example, serve as "hubs," coordinating resources and projects among their satellite schools, affiliated social welfare institutions and media outlets.

By developing relations with senior community leaders within these networks, US policymakers and international development organizations can access a broad cross-section of Pakistanis down to the grassroots level. Using this model, Pakistani development organizations have been able to implement programs in areas where international organizations are unable to operate.

Overview of Regional Trends

Southern Punjab:
- In 2010 and 2011, devastating floods swept through Southern Punjab, disrupting the economy of Pakistan's "bread basket," and displacing thousands of people.
- This region is a major recruiting ground for the Taliban and other militant organizations.

Northern Punjab including the Federal Capital Territory, Islamabad:
- Northern Punjab is relatively safer than southern Punjab due to a high security force presence and its proximity to the capital and military headquarters.
- The region enjoys higher social development indicators (e.g. literacy rates and communications infrastructure) as well as a large volume of civil society organizations through which moderates can conduct CVE campaigns.
- Several major think tanks, internationally funded development organizations, and peace NGOs are based in the capital city, Islamabad.

Overview of Regional Trends (continued from previous page)

Azad Jammu and Kashmir (AJK):
- The region, which has historically been a point of contention between India and Pakistan, is economically depressed and its infrastructure is underdeveloped.
- In 2005, a major earthquake occurred near the city of Muzaffarabad in AJK, which killed approximately 86,000 people, and injured more than 69,000.
- Charitable social welfare organizations with ties to radical groups (e.g. Jamaat-ud-Dawa) receive popular support because of humanitarian assistance they have provided to earthquake victims.
- Given the ongoing land dispute between Pakistan and India, many Pakistani Kashmiris are sympathetic to anti-Indian militant groups such as Lashkar-e-Taiba.

Swat, Khyber Pakhtunkhwa Province:
- Once a popular vacation destination, the mountainous region of Swat has been devastated by recent floods and militant insurgencies.
- Since 2007, the Pakistan military has waged largely successful counter-insurgency operations against the Tehreek e-Taliban Pakistan (TTP) in Swat, and has established de-radicalization camps for at-risk youth/former militants.
In June 2012, following a major ambush of Pakistani soldiers, the TTP threatened to recapture Swat, and take control of Pakistan. Civil society activists fear that militants may return if the region is not strengthened by "hold and build" efforts.

Federally Administered Tribal Areas (FATA):
- FATA, a semi-autonomous tribal region along Pakistan's northwestern border with Afghanistan, has historically been one of the most under-developed territories.
- Militants have taken advantage of the poor economic situation in the region to recruit youth. Militant groups regularly attack moderate mosques and madrassas, as well as government schools.
- Local defensive *lashkars* (civil armed militias) have been formed in response, but lack substantial support from the government.

Sindh:
- Socio-political strife is largely concentrated in Karachi where ethnic tensions have led to violence.
- The frequency of terrorist attacks is lower in interior Sindh compared to other provinces, partly due to local traditions of religious tolerance and interfaith worship at Sufi shrines. Policy analysts however project that the region will become the next major recruiting ground for militant groups exploiting socio-economic inequalities.

Baluchistan:
- This sparsely populated and underdeveloped province has been destabilized by decades of inter-ethnic/tribal conflicts and violent separatist movements.
- The provincial capital, Quetta, is believed to be the headquarters of the Afghan Taliban leadership, the "Quetta Shura."

THE SIGNIFICANCE OF PAKISTAN'S TRADITIONAL MUSLIM NETWORKS

A common question in the debate on countering violent extremism is "Where is the moderate Muslim voice on this critical issue?" This report seeks to address this question. While we interviewed both faith-based and non-faith based groups, our analysis focuses largely on faith-based organizations and what we refer to as "traditional Muslim networks." These networks are comprised of Sunni and Shi'a faith-based organizations that promote peace and social cohesion, and unconditionally reject terrorism, suicide bombings, and other extremist ideologies and tactics advocated by the Taliban. It is important to note however, that these groups are not necessarily pro-American. While some traditional Muslim networks have issued public statements against US interference in Pakistan, they categorically reject the use of terrorism to accomplish political objectives.

In Muslim communities throughout the world, faith-based organizations, community centers and their affiliate institutions play an integral role in developing positive social networks by offering communities a central venue for education, spiritual development, cultural celebrations, and social services. By virtue of their ability to bring communities together to address contemporary issues within a religious paradigm, these institutions are instrumental in building community resilience against extremism.

There are several overarching factors that explain the significance of traditional Muslim networks in countering radical ideologies.

First, traditional Muslim networks are able to build resilience by establishing educational institutions that provide communities a moderate foundation of Islam that unconditionally rejects the Taliban's ideology. Religious institutions that facilitate information and communication such as book publishers, journals, newspapers, and radio stations are often linked to major schools and madrasas which serve as "hubs" that coordinate resources and projects. For example, in the city of Bhera in northern Punjab, the Dar ul-Uloom Muhammadia Ghousia acts as an umbrella institution which oversees a network of over 250 schools across Pakistan, as well as one of Pakistan's largest religious publishing houses "Zia ul-Quran," and the major social-welfare organization "Zia ul-Ummah Foundation."

Second, for at-risk populations, traditional Muslim institutions are critical places for conducting counter-extremism as well as de-radicalization programming such as "anti-terror camps."[18] For example, when community members in Rahim Yar Khan in southern Punjab became concerned about several young men who had radicalized, the parents of the young men approached a local madrasa to request an intervention. One of the community's well-respected scholars met with the young men to explain that terrorism had no place in Islam. "It wasn't a simple process," he explained. "We argued back and forth for days, but eventually the boys learned that their concept of jihad was doctrinally inaccurate."[19] Such interventions are occasionally taped and informally shared with other at-risk youth. Their efficacy is due to the fact that religious scholars within traditional Muslim networks are familiar with arguments employed by radical clerics and counter them point-by-point within a sound, theological framework.

Third, religious leaders operate at the grassroots level and are intimately aware of dynamics within their communities. As such, they can rapidly identify radicalization and know how to intervene appropriately. In a village near Bhera, for example, a father learned that his son was being influenced by a radical recruiter to believe that he would enter paradise if he became a suicide bomber. The father turned to

---

[18] "Anti-terror camps" refer to structured group workshops which address theological issues surrounding violence and jihad. They are often incorporated into larger curriculums on scriptural interpretation and Islamic law.
[19] Interview with a community leader in Multan, July 13, 2011.

teachers at the local Dar ul-Uloom, who advised him on how to publically cast doubt on the recruiter's religious credentials by delegitimizing him in their conservative community. The father rescued his son by exposing the radical mullah. In a community gathering, he challenged the mullah: "After sending my child to paradise, why don't you send your own son to join him so that mine won't be lonely?" The recruiter eventually relented and was unable to attract additional children from that town.[20]

Others employ a transformative behavioral approach rooted in Sufi meditative traditions which has been applied by theologians throughout Muslim communities across the world. In this approach, at-risk and radicalized individuals pursue a slow process of personal transformation under the guidance of religious scholars through fasting, prayer, meditation, Qur'anic recitation, and consciously exercising compassion and forgiveness towards themselves and others. According to Qamar-ul Huda, through this process, "The heart and mind are gradually transformed toward peace - moving away from greed, egocentric desires, suffering, materialism, and harming others [so that] humans then can act peacefully in the world."[21] Throughout our fieldwork, community members confirmed the effectiveness of this process, especially for rehabilitating youth that demonstrate intolerant or anti-social behavior.

Fourth, because these leaders have earned the trust of their communities, they have the potential to mobilize community members in post-conflict reconstruction and "hold and build efforts." In Swat, for example, local peace committees comprised of community leaders and traditional Muslim scholars were created with the support of the Pakistani military to formulate grassroots strategies to counter the Taliban. When the military initiated its counter-insurgency operations in the town of Bahrain, religious leaders and community elders led the town in painting Pakistani flags on store fronts to demonstrate their support of the state and rejection of Taliban rule. After the military had cleared the area of militants, widespread floods devastated the region in 2010. Entire villages were wiped out and thousands were displaced. The local peace councils were then used to create strategies to build dispensaries, schools and water-supply projects.[22]

Similarly, in Malakand, the administrators of the madrasa Jamia Subhaniyya Rizvia have teamed up with other faith-based social welfare organizations such as the Saylani Welfare Trust, the Barakati Foundation, and Muslim Hands to collect emergency kits at the madrasa and distribute them to internally displaced peoples (IDPs) from Taliban-affected regions in the Khyber-Pakhtunkhwa province. In addition, teams of 15-20 student volunteers distributed over 30 tons of goods donated by the military.[23]

Fifth, we found that traditional Muslim networks are active on every level of society, forming a critical segment of Pakistan's civil society. As such, their religious institutions serve as central channels for disseminating anti-extremism messages to large audiences. Every Friday, for example, mosques attract attendants from a large cross section of the community and are important venues to address sensitive socio-political subjects, particularly for illiterate segments of the population.[24] Furthermore, shrines like Lal Shabaz Qalandar in interior Sindh draw millions of Muslims and non-Muslims from across the country to celebrate spiritual occasions, demonstrating broad interfaith harmony.[25] Major moderate madrasas

---

[20] Interview with Ustadh Shaukut at the Dar ul-Uloom Bhera, Bhera. July 1, 2011.
[21] Qamar ul Huda, *Crescent and Dove: Peace and Conflict Resolution in Islam*. USIP. 2010: page xviii.
[22] Interview with a community organizer in Bahrain, Swat, July 25, 2011.
[23] Interview with Mufti Jamil, Malakand, July 28, 2011.
[24] "Ulama Agents for Social Change: Muslim Scholars Speak for Mothers' Rights," *John Hopkins Bloomberg School of Public Health*, 2010, http://paiman.jsi.com/Resources/Docs/ulama-agents-for-social-change.pdf
[25] Interview with a shrine caretaker, August 23, 2011.

also engage diverse segments of Pakistani society through their satellite campuses. The Dar ul-Uloom Muhammadia Ghousia, for example, is part of a network of schools that provides education to over 25,000 men and women.[26]

Traditional Muslim networks are also often linked to Pakistani policy makers. Several members of the National Assembly and Federal Ministers belong to prominent families within these networks and lawmakers such as MNA Faisal Karim Kundi, the Deputy Speaker of the House, have defeated pro-Taliban candidates with the support of traditional Muslim groups in their constituencies.[27]

Evaluating the Success of CVE Efforts

Evaluating the efficacy of CVE programs is a common challenge in the field.[28] In this study, WORDE defined effective programs to be those that not only disengaged individuals from violence, but also transformed the person's radical mindset by refuting the extreme ideologies that motivated them to pursue militancy.

Given that ideological shifts take place over time, psychological assessments can be administered several months after an intervention to evaluate whether a radicalized individual has transformed. Although this approach could yield quantifiable data, in countries such as Pakistan where radicalization is triggered by a number of causes specific to each region, ethnicity, or community, a streamlined survey approach would be difficult to implement and would yield limited results.

A subjective, interpersonal approach is therefore best suited for understanding how peace-building has affected individuals and communities' lives in Pakistan. An effective means to measure this is the "Most Significant Change methodology" (MSC) in which subjects are asked how their life and worldview has changed after an intervention. MSC is also well-suited to monitor and evaluate grassroots initiatives that do not have predefined outcomes against which to evaluate. This is the approach that WORDE field researchers utilized in this study. This report highlights anecdotal evidence of successful peace-building initiatives.

---

[26] Interview with Ustadh Shaukut at the Dar ul-Uloom Bhera, Bhera. July 1, 2011.
[27] Interview with MNA Faisal Karim Kundi, August 2, 2011.
[28] See for example, Angel Rabasa, Stacie Pettyjohn, Jeremy Ghez, and Christopher Boucek, "Deradicalizing Islamist Extremists," *RAND Corporation,* 2010.

THE RISE OF EXTREMIST GROUPS IN PAKISTAN

Despite the predominance of traditional Muslim networks in Pakistan, extremist movements are gaining strength due to major regional political trends that have developed over the past thirty years. This section explores these historical trends and the methods by which extremist groups seek to augment their influence in society today.

THE AFGHAN WAR AND ITS AFTERMATH (1979-2001)

In 1979, the Iranian Revolution sparked a sectarian proxy war between Saudi Arabia and Iran, which continues until today, with each state vying to increase its influence over Pakistani society. For example, Iran supports a number of Shi'a political movements in Pakistan to advocate for greater Shi'a rights and representation in federal Islamic institutions, and Saudi Arabia funds the development and expansion of conservative Sunni madrasas.[29] These schools glorify militant jihad, denounce pluralism and propagate intolerant beliefs such as *takfirism*.[30] In the 1980s these foreign funded madrasas were prime institutions to recruit young Pakistanis on ideological grounds to fight against the Soviets in Afghanistan. Today they continue to serve as breeding grounds for terrorist movements against the West.[31]

Foreign support[32] of conservative religious institutions and the anti-Soviet mujahideen had several unintended consequences in Pakistan including the propagation of radical ideologies and the influx of weapons into the region. New militant groups have also developed such as the Sipah-e Sahaba Pakistan/Lashkar-e Jhangvi (LeJ) and the Sipah-e Muhammad Pakistan. While some extremist organizations seek to "Islamicize" society through political and ostensibly non-violent means, organizations such as LeJ have fomented a culture of intolerance, and have popularized the use of violence to achieve socio-political objectives.[33]

Extremist institutions have continued to receive a steady stream of foreign support, enabling them to rapidly expand their institutional presence throughout Pakistan. According to a recent Wikileak, nearly $100 million is annually funneled to radical madrasas in southern Punjab alone from Gulf States, creating a critical support base for global terrorist groups.[34] Despite this, sustained and coordinated efforts have not been made at the international level to trace and stop the sources of funding.[35]

---

[29] *International Crisis Group Asia Report Number* 216, December 12, 2011.

[30] Takfirism is the practice of declaring anyone who does not conform to their belief system – including Shi'a and Sufi Sunni Muslims -- as *kufar* or non-believers, subject to punishment by death.

[31] Hedieh Mirahmadi, Mehreen Farooq and Waleed Ziad, "Traditional Muslim Networks: Pakistan's Untapped Resource in the Fight Against Terrorism," WORDE Report, May 2010.

[32] G. Kepel, Jihad: The Trail of Political Islam, London: Belknap Press, 2002; Coll, S. *Ghost Wars: The Secret History of the CIA, Afghanistan, and bin Laden, from the Soviet Invasion to September 11, 2001*. New York: The Penguin Press, 2004:. 65

[33] Mariam Abou Zahab, "The Regional Dimension of Sectarian Conflicts in Pakistan," in *Pakistan: Nationalism without a Nation?* Edited by Christophe Jaffrelot, Manohar Publishers & Distributors, New Delhi, 2002.

[34] Walsh, D. "Wikileaks cables portrays Saudi Arabia as a cash machine for terrorists." *The Guardian* <http://www.guardian.co.uk/world/2010/dec/05/wikileaks-cables-saudi-terrorist-funding>

[35] "2008: Extremist Recruitment on the Rise in South Punjab Madrassahs," Dawn, May 22, 2011, http://dawn.com/2011/05/22/2008-extremist-recruitment-on-the-rise-in-south-punjab-madrassahs/

EXTREMIST GROUPS AFTER 9-11 (2001-2012)

While the Pakistani intelligence apparatus has allegedly supported militant groups for geo-strategic interests, extremists are increasing their influence in Pakistan well-beyond the state's control today. Given the large body of literature on state-sponsored extremism,[36] this report will focus instead on the means by which these groups have expanded independent of the state.

Since 2001, most Pakistani militant factions have relied on intimidation tactics to coerce populations to support their movements. Numerous anti-Taliban institutions, including dozens of Sufi shrines and madrasas, have been bombed. To protect themselves, moderate shrines and mosques have become so heavily fortified that attendance is at an all-time low.

In much of the tribal areas bordering Afghanistan, countless moderate religious leaders have been targeted for speaking out against the Taliban, and others have been forced to flee the region. In the Swat Valley, for example, the Swati Taliban carried out a systematic campaign to silence dissent. In 2010, the Taliban killed Dr. Muhammad Farooq Khan, one of Swat's most respected public intellectuals and the first Vice Chancellor of the Swat Islamic University. Dr. Farooq had written several works that condemned suicide bombing and Islamist militancy and had criticized the Taliban on television.[37] Similarly, a revered Sufi leader of Matta, Pir Samiullah, was killed along with 63 of his followers, and was hung from a tree for four days.[38] In Kabal, the popular scholar Maulana Hamidullah was murdered during his evening prayers after he openly criticized the Taliban in one of his weekly sermons.[39]

Anti-Taliban political figures in the frontier are also routinely targeted. In 2007, the popular District Nazim, Miangul Asfandyar Amirzeb, was killed in a roadside improvised explosive device (IED). Amirzeb was the grandson of the former ruler, or Wali, of Swat. In 2010, militants assassinated Mian Rashid Hussain, the son of Mian Iftikhar Hussain, a known outspoken critic of the Taliban.[40] Similarly, in Khyber Agency, MNA Shaykh Nur al Haq Qadri, one of the most influential religious scholars in FATA, has had 16 members of his family murdered or kidnapped by militants.[41]

According to Dr. Javed Hussain, a former MNA and a leading Shi'a religious figure of Parachinar in Kurram Agency in FATA, the new generation of militants has broken all cultural or traditional mores by targeting women and children in their attacks.[42] Prior to our interview, a newly wed schoolteacher in his town was kidnapped along with her husband. Four days before the Eid holidays they were both killed by the Taliban, and the husband's body was found mutilated.

---

[36] See for example, Daniel Byman, "The Changing Nature of State Sponsorship of Terrorism," *Brookings Analysis Paper*, Number 16, May 2008; and
Ashley J. Telis, "Pakistan and the War on Terror: Conflicted Goals, Compromised Performances," *Carnegie Endowment for International Peace,* 2008.
[37] Robert Mackey, "A Moderate Voice is Silenced," *The New York Times*, October 7, 2010.
http://thelede.blogs.nytimes.com/2010/10/07/a-moderate-voice-is-silenced-in-pakistan/?ref=asia
[38] "Miscreants Desecrate Graves in Matta," *The News,* August 18, 2011,
http://www.thenews.com.pk/TodaysPrintDetail.aspx?ID=63421&Cat=2
[39] Interview with a community organizer from Swat, July 26, 2011.
[40] Iftikhar Firdous, "Mian Iftikhar's Son Laid to Rest," *The Express Tribune,* July 25, 2010,
http://tribune.com.pk/story/30893/mian-iftikhars-son-gunned-down/
[41] Interview with MNA Shaykh Nur al Haq Qadri, Islamabad, July 11, 2011.
[42] Interview with Dr. Javed Hussain, September 13, 2011.

Charitable organizations with ties to radical groups such as Jamaat-ud-Dawa exploit poverty as a recruitment tool. Facing increasing unemployment and political disillusionment, youth are by far the most important demographic for Taliban recruiters. This is a particularly disturbing trend considering that an estimated 102 million Pakistanis, or 59% of the population, are under the age of 24.[43] Some extremist groups offer youth employment in which they can earn thousands of rupees a day. Throughout southern Punjab, families reported that extremist madrasa recruiters had offered their children free education, housing, and food. Many of these children were never heard from again, and are believed by community members to have been sold to militant outfits at $3,000 per head.[44] In a country where the GDP per capita is about $2800,[45] communities are finding it increasingly difficult to take a prominent stand against militants.

Extremist groups also seek to expand their influence at the institutional level, waging a fierce battle over the ownership of existing religious institutions that have historically rejected terrorism. Our team interviewed mosque caretakers and madrasa administrators from Peshawar to Karachi, who explained that mosques are being seized through armed conflict at an unprecedented rate. Community activists claimed that in Karachi alone, radicals have overtaken hundreds of mosques. Others are being taken through "legal" means, by manipulating the registration process and changing mosque ownership, creating legal associations untainted by the names of banned groups. In some areas extremists even mask themselves as moderates. Once they have won the trust of a congregation they begin the process of disseminating their radical teachings.

Militants have also capitalized on socio-political grievances to gain support. In the Swat Valley, for example, the militant cleric Maulana Fazlullah established an illegal radio station through which he led people to believe that the Government of Pakistan and the US were orchestrating a grand conspiracy to destroy Islam.[46] He targeted his broadcasts to uneducated populations in remote villages who were unable to distinguish religious conservatism from violent extremism. A charismatic radio personality, Fazlullah presented himself as a liberator, exploiting age-old tensions between laborers, farmers, and the rich landowning class. Given the mounting frustration over drone strikes in the region, many Swatis readily bought into his narrative, and women in the area were known to have donated hundreds of millions of rupees of gold from their dowries to support Fazlullah's purportedly holy cause.[47] According to Dr. Fareeha Paracha, the Director of Pakistan's de-radicalization school Sabaoon, although militants such as Fazlullah have been pushed out of the region, without additional economic opportunities in the region, 15,000-20,000 children in the Swat Valley remain at risk of falling into the hands of extremist recruiters.[48]

---

[43] Moeed Yusuf, "Youth and the Future" in *The Future of Pakistan*, edited by Stephen Cohen, *Brookings*, Washington DC,
2011.
[44] Waleed Ziad and Mehreen Farooq, "The Battle for Pakistan's Soul," *Foreign Policy*, September 1, 2011, http://afpak.foreignpolicy.com/posts/2011/09/01/the_battle_for_pakistans_soul
[45] "Pakistan," *CIA World Factbook*, May 9, 2012, https://www.cia.gov/library/publications/the-world-factbook/geos/pk.html (Accessed June 9, 2012).
[46] Interview with a madrasa educator at Saidu Sharif, Swat, July 25, 2011.
[47] Interview with a community organizer in Swat, July 26, 2011.
[48] "Countering Radicalization and Violent Extremism in Pakistan," *US Institute of Peace* Event, May 9, 2011.

Extremist Groups Operating in Pakistan

There are dozens of well-established extremist institutions operating throughout Pakistan created by former mujahedeen or sympathizers that are functioning at five different levels:

1. Terrorist organizations that sanction jihad without official state approval, and inflict civilian casualties through the use of terror tactics such as suicide bombings. These include the Pakistani Taliban, Lashkar-e Islam, Harkat-ul-Mujahideen, Jaish-e-Muhammad, and Lashkar e-Taiba.

2. Organizations that wage jihad against military and security forces, but are opposed to the use of suicide bombings and in some cases violence against innocent civilians. These include pro-Taliban organizations and Kashmiri groups such as Al-Badr, and Al-Umar Mujahideen.

3. Sectarian militant organizations that use violence against those who do not conform to their particular belief system. These include the Sunni Sipah-e Sihaba / Lashkar e-Jhangvi and the Shi'a Sipah-e Muhammad Pakistan.

4. Fundraising and development organizations that are not directly involved in militancy but provide financial support. This includes organizations such as Jamaat-ud-Dawa, Al–Akhtar Trust, Al-Rashid Trust, and Ummah Tamir-e Nau.

5. Non-violent Deobandi / Salafi groups who do not unconditionally condemn violent extremism. They may denounce terrorism in Pakistan but will include a caveat in their explanations (e.g. allowing for jihad in Afghanistan). These groups generally espouse an intolerant interpretation of Islam. While they might not be directly involved in militancy, they lay the ideological foundation for violence and may provide tacit support for militant outfits. These include educational, political and social-welfare organizations affiliated with Jamaat Islami, Jamiat Ulema-e Islam (JUI-F and JUI-S), and Jamiat Ahl-e Hadith. Such groups are often not considered "extremist" because they are well rooted into Pakistan's social fabric. Because these groups capitalize on political grievances (e.g. drone attacks and the war in Afghanistan), their influence in society is increasing alongside frustration with US involvement in the region.

GOVERNMENT-LED COUNTER EXTREMISM EFFORTS

There have been a number of policies and reforms implemented to address the threat of extremism both at the government and civil society level. The Government of Pakistan (GoP) has enacted initiatives across key sectors such as education, media, economic development and security. Nonetheless, the GoP's record on countering extremism has been mixed, reflecting many challenges including weak governance capacity, civil-military divides, domestic political constraints, conflicting strategic objectives, as well as economic obstacles. In addition, successive Pakistani governments – both civilian and military – have relied to varying extents on the support of certain religious political parties and leaders for political legitimacy. This has constrained the will and capacity of the GoP to implement robust policies that affect religious groups.

The following section highlights milestones in the GoP's approach to countering extremism, and includes recommendations presented by civil society leaders. Without an improvement of existing achievements, community leaders noted that progress at the civil society level would be limited.

MADRASA REFORMS

Building off of a 2002 ordinance, in 2008 President Musharraf issued the Madrasa Registration Ordinance to regulate the country's autonomous madrasa system. The reforms prohibited schools from teaching radical curricula and required all madrasas to register in a national database. According to official data, the majority of the 20,000 seminaries in Pakistan have been registered.[49] Still, educators complain that the registration process lacks proper oversight. In southern Punjab for example, extremist groups are believed to have manipulated the registration process by recording moderate institutions under their names.[50]

The 2008 reforms also required madrasas to streamline textbooks and expand their course offerings to include liberal arts and science in their curriculum. Madrasa educators were initially hesitant to enforce these reforms and cede their autonomy to the state. However, in 2010 the government entered into an agreement with the Ittehad Tanzeemat-i-Madaris Pakistan (ITMP), an umbrella organization of the madrasa oversight boards, to oversee the implementation of madrasa curriculum reforms. A key provision of the agreement stipulates, "No madrasa shall teach or publish any literature which promotes militancy or spreads sectarianism."[51] Despite steps outlined in the agreement to implement further reforms, progress has been delayed purportedly due to bureaucratic obstacles.[52]

---

[49] Azam Khan, "Madrassa Reforms: Broadening horizons for Seminary Students" *Tribune*, October 19, 2011, http://tribune.com.pk/story/276915/madrassa-reforms-broadening-horizons-for-seminary-students/

[50] Interview with religious community leader in Multan, July 13, 2011.

[51] Syed Irfan Reza, "Accord for Introducing Contemporary Subjects in Medrassahs Signed," *Dawn*, October 8, 2010, http://dawn.com/2010/10/08/accord-for-introducing-contemporary-subjects-in-madressahs-signed/

[52] Khawar Ghumman, "Madressah Reforms Making no Headway," *Dawn*, January 13, 2011. http://dawn.com/2011/01/13/madressah-reforms-making-no-headway-2/
Saba Imtiaz, "Is the Road to Madrassa Reform Going Anywhere?" *Dawn*, March 26, 2011, http://tribune.com.pk/story/137860/is-the-road-to-madrassa-reform-going-anywhere/

ECONOMIC DEVELOPMENT

Economic development, particularly with respect to employment opportunities for youth, is viewed as an essential component to countering radicalization. However, Pakistan's economic performance in recent years has been poor. Power and gas shortages, inflation, price hikes for basic commodities, and reduced investment in job-creating industries are contributing to further economic disparities.[53]

In October 2008, the Pakistani Parliament unanimously adopted a 14-point anti-terrorism resolution that acknowledged the role of economic development in conflict regions such as FATA and Baluchistan as keys to stabilizing the region. It also urged the government to develop regional trade agreements. In bilateral talks this year, the government stressed its desire for the U.S. to offer alternative trade concessions, and in 2011 Pakistan and India commenced landmark bilateral trade discussions that have achieved unprecedented progress.[54]

GOOD GOVERNANCE REFORMS

The integral link between good governance and countering violent extremism is well acknowledged among experts and policymakers.[55] In particular, the absence of robust democratic institutions and dysfunctional civil-military relations has inhibited the Pakistani state's ability to implement effective counterterrorism and counterinsurgency policies.[56]

President Zardari's government has enacted important reforms in recent years. For example, the passage of the 18th amendment to the Constitution of Pakistan in 2010 reversed many of the controversial reforms promulgated under Presidents Musharraf and Zia ul-Haq. The bill removed the power of the President to dissolve the Parliament unilaterally and devolved federal ministries in key sectors including education and health to the provinces, in an effort to improve resource allocation and oversight.[57] In addition, the extension of the Political Parties Act to the FATA was an important step towards integrating the isolated region into the mainstream socio-political spheres of Pakistan.[58] Despite the capacity of these initiatives to improve the political infrastructure of Pakistan, success has been limited without robust anti-corruption reforms.

MEDIA

Pakistani media has flourished in the past decade, undergoing a dramatic transformation from high levels of state control to a diverse and largely independent sector ushered in by President Musharraf's liberalization policies. The expansion of Pakistan's media is generally recognized as a positive factor in developing Pakistan's civil society and promoting public awareness on key national security issues. In 2009 for example, the media became increasingly critical of the Taliban insurgency in Swat. Notwithstanding these reforms, a government-led strategy is required to ensure protection for

---

[53] Hasan Askari Rizvi, "Reversing Pakistan's Drift Toward Radicalism," *The German Marshal Fund of the United States,* February 23, 2011,
[56] Shahbaz Rana, "Pakistan to Propose Alternative Trade Schemes to the US," *Express Tribune,* March 9, 2012.
[55] Ahmed Rashid, "After 9/11, Hate begat Hate," *The New York Times*, September 10, 2011.
[56] Amil Khan. "Beyond a Military Solution for Pakistan," *Foreign Policy*, August 6, 2010.
[57] K. Alan Kronstadt, "Pakistan: Key Current Issues and Developments," *Congressional Research Service*, June 1, 2010. P. 55-56.
[58] Afrasiab Khattak. "Reforms in Fata." *Dawn*, October 25, 2011.

journalists. Moreover, ethics and accountability standards are needed to reduce sensationalist coverage and encourage responsible, accurate reporting.[59]

SECURITY

The GoP has taken several steps to curtail the operations of extremists. As early as August 14, 2001, following a series of attacks on Shi'a mosques and Christian churches, President Musharraf announced a nationwide strategy to prohibit sectarian militants from operating and banned eight major militant groups.[60] In addition, the Pakistani military has led counter insurgency operations in Swat in the Khyber Pakhtunkhwa Province and six of the seven agencies in the Federally Administered Tribal Areas (FATA). According to official estimates, Pakistan has suffered a greater number of civilian and military deaths combined than any of the other 49 allies in the regional conflict.[61] Additional measures, however, are required to prevent militant groups from operating under new names and providing safe havens for Taliban commanders.[62]

OFFICIAL DE-RADICALIZATION CAMPS

Following the counter-insurgency operations in Swat, the military has established several de-radicalization centers.[63] The Mashal center and the Sabaoon School were created to rehabilitate young men recruited by the Taliban to support their operations.[64] Participants are offered psychological counseling and religious reeducation, as well as vocational training. A "whole of community" approach is also utilized to monitor participants through telephone follow-ups and visits to families.[65] A third de-radicalization camp, Phytiom, focuses on older recruits who have spent significant time on the frontlines of the insurgency. According to the Director of Hum Pakistani Foundation, Dr. Fareeha Peracha, who evaluates the progress of participants, the de-radicalization efforts have been largely successful. The GoP plans to open two additional de-radicalization centers in Bajaur Agency and Tank, an area adjacent to South Waziristan.[66] In addition to these efforts, the military recently established a radio station, *FM 96*, to counter terrorist propaganda in the Swat valley. The station not only plays popular songs, but also features talk shows and debates on contemporary socio-political issues. Currently broadcasting in 16 cities, the military plans to expand the station to 44 cities and towns, including regions within FATA.[67]

---

[59] Hannah Byam and Christopher Neu, "Covering and Countering Extremism in Pakistan's Developing Media," *United States Institute of Peace*, March 2011.

[60] These groups include Jaish-i-Mohammad, Sipha-i-Sahaba, Lashker-i-Jhangvi, Lashkre-e-Taiba, Tehrik-i-Nifaz-i-Shariat Mohammadi, Tehrik-i-Fiqa Jafriya, Tehrik-i-Taliban Pakistan (TTP), Sipha Mohammad, and Harkat-ul-Mujahedin
"BBC News South Asia. Pakistan Profile," updated January 17, 2012. http://www.bbc.co.uk/news/world-south-asia-12966786

[61] "Rebuff to White House Report: Military Satisfied with Counter-terror Efforts." *The Express Tribune*, April 9, 2011.
Ali Abbas and Shemrez Nauman, "Countering Radical Ideology," *The Friday Times*, July 22, 2011.

[62] Michael Hirsh, "American Ally, American Adversary: Our Worsening Pakistan Problem," *The Atlantic,* May 30, 2012,

[63] "Pakistan's Youth Taken back from the Taliban," *BBC News South Asia*, October 8, 2010.

[64] "Army Introduces De-radicalisation Cenre in Swat," *Dawn Multimedia*, April 25, 2012. http://dawn.com/2012/04/25/mashal-de-radicalisation-centre/

[65] "Countering Radicalization and Violent Extremism in Pakistan," *US Institute of Peace* Event, May 9, 2011.

[66] Zulfiqar Ali, "De-radicalisation Centres being set up in Bajaur, Tank," *Dawn Newspaper*, January 21, 2012.

[67] Aijaz Maher, "Pakistan's Army Steps up Radio Wars," *BBC Urdu,* August 14, 2012, http://www.bbc.co.uk/news/world-asia-18766713

CIVIL SOCIETY LEVEL EFFORTS TO COUNTER EXTREMISM

In place of a comprehensive government-led strategy to counter extremism, Pakistan's civil society is faced with the responsibility to fill in the gaps for the immediate and short term. CSO efforts have aimed both to increase awareness and counter radicalization at the national and local levels.

PUBLIC AWARENESS CAMPAIGNS

Our research indicates that generating public awareness on violent extremism is critical to empowering the Government of Pakistan with the appropriate political capital to counter these threats effectively. CSOs across the country are developing awareness through a multitude of platforms and mediums including the media, public rallies, conferences, poster campaigns and online petitions. The strength of these grassroots, locally-driven efforts lies in their context-specific approaches and ability to provide a legitimate counter-narrative to violent extremism. The following sections present examples of public awareness initiatives and their limitations.

Conferences & Seminars

Conferences are frequently convened by civil society leaders to create strategies and slogans for anti-terror campaigns as well as to mobilize support among various segments of the population. For example, when militants were gaining ground in Swat in 2009, religious figures from across the country convened the landmark "Istehkam-e Pakistan Conference" in Lahore. Community leaders from Khyber Pakhtunkhwa Province briefed participants on the extent of atrocities committed by the Taliban. During the conference, Pakistan's leading ulema unanimously pledged their support for a military intervention in Swat, and approached the government to initiate counter-insurgency operations. Afterwards, religious scholars returned to their communities and briefed congregations across urban and rural areas. According to civil society leaders, without public support, it would have been difficult for the military to take the appropriate decisive action.[68]

Secular groups are also launching initiatives calling for peace, moderation and greater government action to promote the rule of law in Pakistan's urban centers. Citizens for Democracy (CFD), a coalition of professional groups, NGOs, trade unions, and political parties opposed to the misuse of religion in politics, recently held a petition campaign. In one day, residents of Karachi posted 15,000 letters to senior political leaders calling for an end to violence and lawlessness and the protection of minorities.[69]

Youth are also playing an increasingly visible role in raising awareness among students and young professionals. For example, Bargad, a youth-development NGO based in Gujranwala, Punjab, hosted the four-day "All Pakistan Student Leaders Conference" in July 2009 that brought together 65 student leaders to develop strategies to challenge the influence of extremist groups on college campuses. Bargad also invited young parliamentarians to discuss civic activism and political empowerment strategies.[70] According to the Deputy Speaker of the House, Faisal Kundi and MNA Donya Aziz, leaders of

---

[68] Waleed Ziad and Mehreen Farooq, "Evicting the Taliban from Swat," *Foreign Policy*, November 2, 2011, http://afpak.foreignpolicy.com/posts/2011/11/02/evicting_the_taliban_from_swat
[69] "Pakistani Women: A Critical Resource for Security and Stability," *USIP Roundtable Event*, April 24, 2012.
[70] Phone interview with Sabiha Shaheen, December 12, 2011.

the Young Parliamentarians Caucus (YPC), the YPC is planning debates in rural and urban universities to engage students in addressing sensitive issues including extremism.[71]

Finally, tribal communities are convening jirgas (assemblies of elders) to address Talibanization. At the height of the Taliban insurgency, Bushra Gohar, a member of the National Assembly of Pakistan from Khyber Pakhtunkhwa Province, convened jirgas of Swati activists. "The problems of extremism in Swat – and across the frontier - were entirely unknown to the public in Pakistan's major cities," she explained. "Through our jirgas, we devised strategies to raise an awareness of the problem in Islamabad."[72]

Public Rallies

Public rallies and demonstrations are another channel through which Pakistani CSOs are raising awareness and promoting collective action. In 2009, the Islamabad-based think tank, the Center for Innovative Research, Collaboration and Learning (CIRCLe) organized a 25,000 man National Flag Day March in 2009 to demonstrate support for the counterinsurgency operations in the Swat Valley. The march brought together various elements of civil society, from conservative Muslim groups to the Christian Progressive Movement of Pakistan.[73]

Women's and human rights groups have also organized public campaigns. In April 2007, the Women's Action Front organized the rally in Lahore "Say No to Talibanisation, Say No to Religious Extremism."[74] Similarly, the NGO Shirkat Gah[75] frequently protests violence against minorities. In May 2010, following attacks on two Ahmedi mosques, activists from the women's NGO Shirkat Gah carried banners throughout Karachi featuring messages condemning violence against religious minorities of Pakistan.

> Women play a critical role in peace-building. As the mothers of conflict-affected youth, and the wives of militant commanders, women have witnessed first-hand how conflict has affected their communities. In addition, because they have unique access to communities, they can help bridge divergent groups. As a result, they are powerful change agents that are uniquely positioned to change hearts and minds.

Pakistan's youth are also promoting awareness of the threat of extremism. For example, the Youth Peace Network established by the Sustainable Peace and Development Organization (SPADO) has organized youth rallies to denounce violence involving students throughout the country, from Karachi to Peshawar. In 2010, SPADO held a "Peace Walk" to protest gun violence at Peshawar University, in which 500 students participated.[76] Similarly, last August, Bargad organized a Youth Mela (festival) for Peace to commemorate the UN International Year of the Youth. Activities included a debate competition entitled, "Youth Can Stop Terrorism."

---

[71] Interview with MNA Faisal Karim Kundi, Islamabad, August 2, 2011.
[72] Interview with Bushra Gohar, Islamabad, July 11, 2011
[73] Interview with Peer Mudassir Shah, Rawalpindi, June 30, 2011.
[74] Ali Waqar, "Thumbs Down on Talibanization," *Daily Times*, April 20, 2007, http://www.dailytimes.com.pk/default.asp?page=2007\04\20\story_20-4-2007_pg13_1
[75] "Pakistan: Shirkat Gah Joins Protests Against Killing of Ahmedis in Lahore and Karachi," *Women Living Under Muslim Laws,* June 3, 2010, http://www.wluml.org/node/6372
[76] Interview with Reza Shah Khan, Islamabad, August 5, 2011.

Moderate madrasas have also encouraged students to participate in anti-terror rallies. For example, after Lahore's landmark Sufi shrine, Data Darbar, was bombed in 2010, students at the nearby Jamia Nizamia Rizvia were given the day off from classes to participate in demonstrations denouncing all forms of terrorism.[77]

Traditional Media

CSOs are using newspapers, television and radio programs, film, and music to disseminate counter-radical narratives to the Pakistani public. Organizations such as the Institute for War and Peace Reporting (IWPR) are training citizens in journalism. IWPR works in 42 state schools and madrasas across Pakistan's troubled areas, including Swat Valley, Karachi and FATA. Their programs have trained approximately 4,000 secondary school students in basic journalism and public discussion skills.

Internationally acclaimed films and documentaries such as Shoaib Mansoor's *Khuda Kay Liye* and Sharmeen Obaid-Chinoy's *Children of the Taliban* are popular examples of countering militant propaganda. A departure from the typical love-story musicals churned out by Lollywood and Bollywood, *Khuda Kay Liye's* commercial success in Pakistan signaled the broad resonance and appeal of counter-narratives to extremism. In a controversial scene of the film, the celebrated actor Naseeruddin Shah testifies in a courtroom as a progressive Islamic scholar and makes a compelling case against narrow interpretations of Islam promoted by violent extremists.

Social Media

Social media represents the newest platform to expand public awareness campaigns. For example, first-hand accounts and videos featuring the plight of Swatis under the Taliban rule were widely circulated through Facebook, Twitter, and SMS. Video footage of the Taliban flogging a young girl, went viral on YouTube, and generated outrage from a broad cross-section of the public. Similarly, an interview of the Taliban commander Sufi Muhammad in which he simultaneously denounced democracy and Pakistanis was widely used by activists to discredit the Taliban.[78]

More recently, taking inspiration from the Arab Spring, Pakistani youth are also using social media forums such as Twitter and Facebook to promote peace initiatives. Online petitions, such as Amman Ittihad's "Call for Peace" which has received over 17,000 signatures, are urging Pakistanis to foster pluralism and harmony between different faiths and ethnicities. Similarly, Facebook pages such as "A call to youth to bring peace in Karachi" mobilized students from universities to participate in a march against targeted killings in August 2011 when political violence in Pakistan's commercial center had escalated to alarming levels.

---

[77] Interview with Dr. Raghib Naeemi, Lahore, August 10, 2011.
[78] Interviews with community organizers, Swat, July 25-29, 2011.

Case Study of the Sunni Ittihad Council

The Sunni Ittihad Council (SIC), an umbrella of moderate religious Sunni groups associated with the Barelvi school of thought, has organized some of Pakistan's boldest anti-terror public awareness campaigns to date. Their flagship campaign was a "Long March" in 2009 from Islamabad to Lahore to train communities in recognizing and preventing extremism. As part of its Public Diplomacy programs, the US Embassy provided the SIC funding for logistical support of such events.[79]

Over the next two years, as militants increased attacks on Pakistan's moderate religious institutions, the SIC continued to organize anti-terror campaigns. They led political campaigns to defeat extremist candidates, denounced the Taliban in the National Assembly, condemned communal violence, and organized national conferences uniting thousands against extremism. In late July 2011, WORDE interviewed senior SIC leaders who were planning a "Train March" from Karachi to Islamabad on the 10th anniversary of 9/11 to demonstrate sympathy for global victims of terrorism.

Unbeknownst to the public, at the time of our fieldwork, there were fissures amongst the SIC leadership. One faction was positioning the SIC to become a political party to compete in the next general elections. However, several others in the SIC leadership were concerned that this move would politicize the organization and dissolve the unity that they had worked very hard to foster. Eventually, the hardline faction that intended the SIC to become a political entity won and the organization quietly changed direction and leadership.[80]

According to a senior leader of the SIC who has now distanced himself from the SIC, "The 2013 elections have created a polarized environment in which issues are emotionally contested. Extremist parties are utilizing anti-Americanism as an effective rallying point. As a result, moderate candidates are increasingly marginalized. Even moderate candidates such as Imran Khan have sought popular support by criticizing US involvement in the region and drone strikes."

Without effective communications training, parties such as the SIC have hardened their rhetoric to remain popular and relevant. For example, when US Secretary of Defense Panetta threatened unilateral action if Pakistan was unable to crack down on the Haqqani Network, hardline members of the SIC issued a public denunciation of the US. Soon after, the Train March was cancelled and replaced by an anti-American rally. According to a former leader of the SIC who refused to partake in the demonstrations, the SIC has since splintered and can no longer be characterized as an umbrella organization. As a result, moderate religious groups have not executed large-scale public awareness campaigns against violent extremism since the split of the organization.

It is important to note that SIC's initial campaigns enabled Pakistanis to turn against militants at a time when the US-Pakistan alliance desperately needed that public support. Through these initiatives, activists noted that Pakistanis have become increasingly comfortable with discussing the challenges of extremism out in the open. Nonetheless, the recent transformation of the SIC has also raised several questions about US support of religious networks in Pakistan. In the current political climate which is rife with anti-Americanism, the US should weigh the costs and benefits of partnering with organizations that are effective in countering violent extremism as a national security interest, independent of public diplomacy objectives.

---

[79] "US Aided Sunni Ittehad Council for Anti-Taliban Rallies," *The Nation*, January 12, 2012.
[80] "US Aid to Sunni Ittihad Council Backfired," Huma Imtiaz, *The Express Tribune*, January 12, 2012.

COUNTERING VIOLENT EXTREMISM INITIATIVES

In tandem with public awareness campaigns, CSOs have organized initiatives to counter extremism on several levels reflecting the will and capacity of Pakistanis to counter extremism. Some programs denounce violence from a religious perspective. Others focus on countering extremism by denouncing intolerance, advocating for social cohesion and promoting interethnic and inter-cultural harmony. Some groups also operate at the individual level, focusing on developing positive personal characteristics (e.g. anger management and conflict mediation skills). While these efforts are not as visible as the actions of extremist elements within Pakistani society, they have been powerful mechanisms of building community resilience to violence.

Building & Expanding Moderate Religious Schools

Traditional Muslim networks are actively engaged in building and expanding educational institutions to deter families from enrolling their children in radical madrasas. Moderate schools are well positioned to form a bulwark against extremism – by openly rejecting violence and countering radical narratives in their classrooms, they provide a safe place to reinforce positive social norms.

According to community leaders across the country, the mere presence of moderate madrasas can create a frontline defense against radicalization. In FATA, we visited a network of anti-Taliban educational institutions that includes girls' schools. When militants began threatening their flagship school near Peshawar, hundreds of teachers publically pledged never to allow extremism in their campuses.[81]

In Bhera, madrasa instructors at the Dar ul-Uloom explained that in their classrooms there is no ambiguity about militant jihad. One director explained, "Our teachers are instructed to provide traditional Islamic education based on Sufi ethos of tolerance, and moderation. We teach our students that it is not their duty to fight jihad, but to look after the wellbeing of their community." In 2010, the school and its affiliate philanthropic and social welfare organizations distributed hundreds of hygiene kits, established medical facilities for over 7,000 people and rebuilt homes for flood victims.

Given Pakistan's underdeveloped public education system, madrasas are an attractive alternative to private schools because children not only receive a free education, but in many cases they are also provided with free clothing, housing and food. In areas where poverty is a major source of recruitment for militant groups, radical madrasas may act as "feeders" to militant outfits, with some schools even offering 'summer camp' opportunities in training camps across the tribal frontier.[82]

In Multan, we interviewed Pir Arshad Kazmi, a revered religious scholar with a background in philosophy, who provides families in southern Punjab with an alternative to extremist madrasas. Over the past several decades, he has built hundreds of schools with funding from local communities. According to Pir Kazmi, "I realized that if we didn't build these schools, our children would grow up with religious intolerance and a narrow, destructive worldview." His flagship institution, the Jamiya Islamiya Anwar ul-Uloom, is a major madrasa in Multan that oversees a network of schools for boys and girls throughout southern Punjab and northern Sindh.[83]

---

[81] Interview with madrasa educators, Khyber Agency (FATA), July 30, 2011.
[82] Interview with a former official of the National Counter-terrorism Authority, July 11, 2011.
[83] Interview with Pir Kazmi, Multan, July 13, 2011.

Where possible, major madrasas are also offering advanced courses in English, sciences, mathematics and vocational training to prepare students for careers after graduation. The majority of traditional Muslim networks we interviewed said that they have plans and aspirations to expand these services; however, many lack the necessary institutional capacity and funding.

Despite the challenges, in Khyber Pakhtunkhwa and FATA where the funding gap is more apparent than other provinces, vocational centers are also being planned for women. In Malakand, we interviewed the administrators of the Jamia Subhaniyya Rizvia, which oversees a network of satellite schools throughout the tribal areas, and the Swat Valley. The administrators recently completed renovations to provide vocational education to 200 women – a first in the region according to the teachers.[84]

Women are playing a major role in promoting religious education because many feel that their lack of education was exploited by radical clerics. One of the largest challenges for establishing women's madrasas, however, is identifying qualified female instructors.

Addressing this challenge, a new approach is being employed in which women attend short courses from male and female religious scholars online. The Zaynab Academy, for example, offers courses in classical Islamic studies, spirituality as well as guidance in peaceful conflict resolution and developing healthy relationships.

Organizing Anti-Terror Camps

Some schools also offer specially designed seminars to counter radicalization in their communities. Minhaj-ul-Quran International, established by the internationally renowned religious scholar, Dr. Tahir ul-Qadri, has developed anti-terror camps in Pakistan to provide young Muslim men and women with sound religious refutation of extremist tenets.[85] Similarly, in Okara (the hometown of several of the 2008 Mumbai attackers), the Dar ul-Uloom Ashraf al-Madaris Okara organizes seminars on Qur'anic principles of peace and conflict resolution. The school has hundreds of schools within its network across Pakistan, through which they intend to disseminate material from the program.[86] The lectures are also available on YouTube.[87]

There are additional models which pursue a less institutionalized approach. In the tribal frontier, the women's organization, PAIMAN, has established the "Let's Live in Peace Project" in which women and youth are taught mediation and conflict transformation skills. According to the founder, Mossarat Qadeem, teaching women these values provides them the capacity to influence their husbands and sons to disengage from militant organizations. "Depending on the situation," she explained, "we also offer psycho-social counseling, life and livelihood skills and education." PAIMAN has been able to conduct their programs in conservative regions of Pakistan by involving religious scholars at every step.[88]

---

[84] Interview with Mufti Jamil, Malakand, July 28, 2011.
[85] Interview with Jamil Raja, Lahore, June 21, 2011.
[86] Interview with educators at the Dar ul-Uloom Ashraf ul-Madaris Okara, July 16, 2011.
[87] See for example, "Ilm ul Quran Course" on YouTube.
[88] Email interview with Mossarat Qadeem, May 12, 2012.

Promoting Interethnic and Interfaith Social Harmony

In regions facing high levels of militancy such as FATA, Swat and southern Punjab, extremists recruit heavily from undereducated and vulnerable communities. Youth within these communities are easily manipulated into accepting a Manichean outlook on life in which the world is bifurcated into simple, antagonistic categories (e.g. Muslims versus non-Muslims, Pakistanis versus Americans, and good versus evil). To help individuals broaden their mindset, several Pakistani CSOs are providing radicalized youth with basic education in cross-cultural awareness to challenge the intolerant ideologies propagated by extremists.[89]

In order to prevent youth radicalization, Peace Network Pakistan, an advocacy platform of approximately 20 NGOs, is establishing policy recommendations to reform school curricula to include components on peace and conflict resolution.[90] In lieu of a government-mandated curriculum to counter intolerant attitudes, several CSOs have developed their own training manuals and seminars. Bushra Hyder, the Director of the Qadims Lumier School and College in Peshawar has designed and implemented a peace education curriculum that introduces students to cultural and religious diversity and is designed to inculcate compassion and tolerance. Her students have formed a group called "Peace Angels" that organizes hospital field trips to meet with victims of terrorism. According to Ms. Hyder, the program helps students understand that violence cannot solve conflict.[91]

Pakistani civil society organizations are promoting religious freedom, tolerance and social harmony through a number of mechanisms including interfaith cultural celebrations, inter-ethnic dialogues, and conflict mediation.

CSOs are also implementing interfaith dialogues and seminars to counter intolerance. For example, the Pak Turk International School system provides students and their families the necessary tools for conducting interfaith dialogue to deconstruct tribal, cultural, and religious stereotypes that plague Pakistan. Given their success, they have been able to operate in volatile regions such as Quetta and Peshawar where sectarian violence and inter-ethnic tensions are prevalent.[92]

Several organizations across Pakistan are promoting social harmony by organizing intercultural events. In 2011, just months after the Taliban were driven out of the Swat Valley, the Idara Baraye Taleem-o-Taraqi (Center for Education and Development) organized the Simam Festival to celebrate Swat's traditional pluralistic culture that had been proscribed by the Taliban.[93] Similarly, in Lahore, the arts and culture NGO, Hast-o-Neest, promotes works of artisans across the country and celebrates diverse traditions of poetry, music, miniature painting and calligraphy. Activists believe it is important to remind Pakistanis that – contrary to the view of radical Islamists - Islam has historically championed diversity in cultural practices.[94]

---

[89] Kirsten Seymour, "De-Radicalization: Psychologists' War against Militants," *Tribune,* July 17, 2011 http://tribune.com.pk/story/211479/de-radicalising-rehab-psychologists-war-against-militants/
[90] Interview with Sameena Imtiaz, Islamabad, August 12, 2011.
[91] "Pakistani Women: A Critical Resource for Security and Stability," *USIP Roundtable Event*, Washington, DC, April 24, 2012.
[92] Waleed Ziad and Mehreen Farooq, "Pakistan's Most Powerful Weapon," October 21, 2011, http://afpak.foreignpolicy.com/posts/2011/10/21/pakistans_most_powerful_weapon
[93] Interview with Zubair Torwali, Swat, July 27, 2011.
[94] Interview with Taimoor Khan Mumtaz, Lahore, August 10, 2011.

Other organizations are working to bridge relations between Muslim and non-Muslim communities in Pakistan. The Christian Progressive Movement (CPM) of Pakistan, for example, regularly collaborates with Muslim organizations to promote human rights and counter extremism and intolerance. In 2010, CPM partnered with Muslim faith-based organizations to protest Switzerland's ban on mosque minarets and in 2011 CPM joined peaceful protests against Pastor Terry Jones' suggestion to burn Qurans.[95] Similarly, the Taangh Wasaib Organization, an organization led by a Christian woman in southern Punjab, promotes social harmony between Muslim, Christian and Hindu populations by drawing examples from local Sufi poetry and folklore.[96]

Muslim organizations lead similar interfaith efforts reaching out to Pakistan's minority groups. In Lahore, Minhaj-ul-Quran engages their madrasa students in annual Christmas celebrations with Lahore's Christian community.[97] In Makli in Sindh, the NGO Web for Human Development brings together the Muslim and Hindu communities to celebrate the Hindu festival of Holi as well as Sufi Muslim festivals.[98] Other organizations such as Baanhn Beli ("A Friend Forever") improve inter-faith relations by engaging both Muslim and Hindu communities in rural Sindh in their grassroots development work.[99] Although these are successful models, inter-faith and intra-faith engagement in Pakistan is in its nascent stages.

Fatwas & Public Statements

Faith-based organizations use fatwas to denounce terrorism at the theological level within an orthodox framework. These statements are geared towards at-risk individuals who are swayed by religious justifications of violence. Since 9-11, dozens of scholars have issued such fatwas in Urdu and local languages. Dr. Tahir ul-Qadri's 600-page fatwa against terrorism and suicide bombing, which has been translated in English, has received international attention and has become a powerful tool for Pakistani religious scholars to streamline anti-terror talking points.

Other scholars regularly issue verbal proclamations denouncing terrorism – often at great personal risk. In 2006, Dr. Sarfaraz Naeemi, the head of one of Lahore's largest madrasas, issued a fatwa on suicide bombing and organized several anti-Taliban rallies and seminars. The Taliban threatened to stop him on a number of occasions and in 2009, he was assassinated in a suicide attack on his school. According to his son, Dr. Raghib Naeemi, after his father's death, many traditional Muslim networks were empowered to speak out against the Taliban. Today, Dr. Raghib Naeemi carries on his father's message, and frequently appears on television.[100]

---

[95] "The Nexus of Sectarian Conflict and Violent Extremism in Pakistan," *WORDE Roundtable Event,* Washington, DC April 27, 2012.
[96] "Taangh Wasaib Organization," *Insight on Conflict*, http://www.insightonconflict.org/conflicts/pakistan/peacebuilding-organisations/two/ (Accessed June 7, 2012).
[97] Waleed Ziad and Mehreen Farooq, "Out-recruiting Pakistan's Extremists," *Foreign Policy,* February 29, 2011, http://afpak.foreignpolicy.com/posts/2012/02/29/out_recruiting_pakistans_extremists
[98] Interview with Allah Jorio, Makli, August 28, 2011.
[99] Interview with Javed Jabbar, Karachi, August 19, 2011.
[100] Interview with Dr. Raghib Naeemi, Lahore, August 10, 2011.

Public Debates against Extremism

Public lectures and community debates are popular options to counter narratives of extremist groups. In these venues, religious scholars and skilled orators from madrasas and mosques employ verses from the Quran, stories of the Prophets, and historical examples to deconstruct radical interpretations of Islam. In regions of Pakistan like southern Punjab where robust civil society networks exist, public debates and lectures are held on a weekly basis and some featuring prominent speakers are televised or posted on YouTube.[101]

Development NGOS & Building Community Resilience

Another strategy to counter violent extremism is building community resilience through development organizations. Although these organizations do not explicitly teach communities how to counter terrorism, their resource mobilization techniques are used to create bottom-up strategies to address challenges– from countering extremism to countering corruption.

CSOs such as the National Rural Support Programme and Sungi, for example, provide communities with the appropriate communications skills so that when a threat is identified, they can develop a strategy within their community to address the problem using their collective resources. These skills are particularly useful for impoverished, rural, at-risk communities. In rural areas of District Abbotabad, for example, villagers employed tools from Sungi's peace and conflict resolution training to counter extremism. A group of radical clerics had offered to build a mosque for the community on the condition that they could bring their own teachers. Not long after, families were alarmed that their children were being radicalized and the community collectively held the mosque under siege until the clerics were forced out.[102]

Humanitarian Relief

Across Pakistan, poverty has provided fertile ground for jihadist recruitment. Similar to tactics employed by the Lebanese group Hezbollah, militants gain popular support among low-income families by providing free food, medical facilities and education. Pakistani organizations like Jamaat-ud-Dawa (JuD), (the charitable front for the terrorist group Lashkar-e-Taiba), feed off of local economic and political frustrations.[103] Groups like JuD have also gained considerable leverage from the floods that ravaged the country in 2010.

Pakistan's civil society networks are providing an alternative to extremists' humanitarian efforts. For example, Al-Mustafa Welfare Society recently partnered with the World Health Organization (WHO) and Rotary International (RI) to organize public events featuring religious scholars to counter the Taliban's claims that the WHO and RI polio vaccines were a Zionist conspiracy to make the population sterile.

CSOs that do not typically engage in social welfare work are also conducting ad-hoc humanitarian assistance. For example, in the 2010 and 2011 floods, many secular universities and moderate madrasas used their social networks to coordinate food and emergency health kit distribution. In southern Punjab,

---

[101] Waleed Ziad and Mehreen Farooq, "The Battle for Pakistan's Soul," *Foreign Policy*, September 1, 2011, http://afpak.foreignpolicy.com/posts/2011/09/01/the_battle_for_pakistans_soul
[102] Interview with Samina Khan, Islamabad, July 5, 2011.
[103] Interviews with community elders, Kashmir, July 25, 2011.

the Society for Education and Peacebuilding (SEP) partnered with the Jamiya Islamiya Anwar ul-Uloom to coordinate humanitarian relief.[104] By tapping into affiliated madrasa and familial networks, organizers were able to provide assistance to villages off the grid in areas beyond the scope of most international NGOs.

Similarly, madrasas often help international organizations coordinate social welfare activities throughout the country at the grass-roots level. For example, the UK-based Muslim Hands and Muslim Charity both operate in Pakistan in close association with the Dar ul-Uloom in Bhera.

Arts

According to Dean Salima Hashmi at Beaconhouse National University (BNU), art is another powerful medium for countering extremism particularly for young audiences. BNU has engaged students in art projects to promote peace, from chalk graffiti on the streets of Lahore, to designing tee shirts. "For many students from upper-middle class backgrounds," Dr. Hashmi explained, "this was the first time they got involved in public activism."[105]

Art has also been used by CSOs like Pakistan Rising to rehabilitate youth affected by the war in Swat. Capitalizing on the success of such organizations, last August, Former Prime Minister Yousaf Raza Gilani called upon leading Pakistani artists for a "Dialogue with the Prime Minister" to help build a national counter-extremism strategy.[106]

On national television, the widely successful show *Coke Studio* has introduced a new mechanism for peace promotion that appeals to multiple levels of society. Every week on prime-time TV, talented musicians from different regions, socio-economic classes and ethnic groups are brought together on a common platform to perform new music on themes that include tolerance and diversity, often combining modern pop music with traditional poetry and songs.[107]

Street theatre is another popular medium. For example, the Tehrik-e-Niswan (Women's Movement) uses street theater to raise awareness of women's issues from the slums of Karachi to interior Sindh.[108] Similarly, the Pakistan Youth Alliance recently arranged a street theater performance in the Swat Valley at a notorious street corner where the Taliban would hang corpses when they controlled the area. The performance was designed to encourage youth to speak out against extremist ideologies.[109]

---

[104] Interview with Shaykh Tahir, Multan, July 12, 2011.
[105] Interview with Salima Hashmi, Lahore, August 11, 2011.
[106] "PM Seeks Artists' Help with Fighting Extremism," *Daily Times*, July 30, 2011, http://www.dailytimes.com.pk/default.asp?page=2011\07\30\story_30-7-2011_pg7_9
[107] Interview with Zeb Bangash, Lahore, July 17, 2011.
[108] Interview with Sheemah Karmani, Karachi, August 25, 2011.
[109] "Pakistan: The New Radicals," *Al Jazeera*, October 27, 2011, http://www.aljazeera.com/programmes/activate/2011/09/20119415101883395.html

Journalism

Pakistan's new media is rapidly becoming a forum to mainstream controversial issues from domestic violence to radical Islamism. Religious leaders have also developed rapid response mechanisms to denounce terrorism in the media following major suicide attacks. For example, in 2010 when the soup kitchen (*langar*) at the Data Darbar shrine in Lahore was bombed, one of the shrine's imams invited the media and mobilized leaders from different mosques to condemn terrorism.[110]

There are efforts to bring youth into these discourses. Nationwide, the Open Minds Project trains students in schools and madrasas in journalism and conflict reporting. Their students have appeared on national news shows. In conflict-affected regions, the Center for Research and Security Studies also invites students to share their stories on radio stations broadcasting in Kohat, Abbottabad, Peshawar and even Afghanistan.[111] Similarly, radio stations established by religious scholars are critical channels for countering radical narratives. For example, in Malakand the educators at the Jamia Subhaniyya Rizvia established Mustafa FM and the Madyan radio stations to counter "Maulana Radio's" efforts. Most of these stations were short-lived because they lacked resources and could not garner financial support from the government.[112]

Armed Resistance

Some groups directly under attack have resorted to armed resistance. For example, when 30-40 armed gunmen occupied two mosques and a madrasa in Bahawalpur, the community retaliated by first contacting the media, public officials, and law enforcement and staging a public rally. When these efforts failed, 150 community members confronted the militants in a standoff. Other communities are taking more drastic measures.[113]

In the tribal areas, many villages created their own "minuteman-style" militias, or *lashkars* to fend off militants. *Lashkar* organizers from FATA explained that there were unable to maintain these defensive militias without sustained support from the international community and the government. As soon as their support waned, the Taliban systematically assassinated the members of the *lashkars*.[114]

In major urban centers, mainstream groups are now turning to organizations like the Sunni Tehreek for armed protection. Founded over 20 years ago to prevent mosque takeovers by radical militants, the Sunni Tehreek has over 6,000 branches across Pakistan today.[115] Without international support, additional moderate networks are expected to turn to these groups. While terror analysts contend that increasing support for such groups could further destabilize the region,[116] many locals believe instead that the organization provides a safeguard against pro-Taliban groups.

---

[110] Interview with Mufti Ramzan, Lahore, August 11, 2011.
[111] Interview with Sameena Imtiaz, and Imtiaz Gul, Islamabad, August 12, 2011
[112] Interview with Mufti Jamil, Malakand, July 28, 2011.
[113] Waleed Ziad and Mehreen Farooq, "The Battle for Pakistan's Soul," *Foreign Policy,* September 1, 2011, http://afpak.foreignpolicy.com/posts/2011/09/01/the_battle_for_pakistans_soul.
[114] Interviews with community organizers from Khyber Agency (FATA), July 25-29, 2011.
[115] Interview with Sunni Tehreek organizers, Multan, July 14, 2011.
[116] Arif Jamal, "Sufi Militants Struggle with Deobandi Jihadists in Pakistan," *Terrorism Monitor* Volume 9, Issue 8, February 24, 2011.

LIMITATIONS & CHALLENGES

The examples highlighted above provide valuable models for countering extremism, however, Pakistan's civil society faces many challenges in replicating these initiatives to create a sustained national movement. Many Pakistanis are also reluctant to take ownership of the problem. They believe it is solely the US' responsibility to resolve these issues; because in their view extremism has resulted from US involvement in the region. While some Pakistanis are in denial that their communities could be radicalizing, others simply fail to grasp the severity of the issue and believe that terrorist attacks are only isolated incidents, rather than emblematic of a larger, systemic problem.

The most prevalent concern cited by civil society activists is a lack of funding and resources. Most community-based groups do not receive support from international organizations, and rely on small community donations. The lack of manpower further constrains efforts. Volunteers carry out most civil society campaigns, and organizers find it difficult to maintain volunteer commitment in the medium and long-term.

While extremist factions have been developing their institutional capacity since the Afghan War, moderate groups – both faith-based and secular - are for all practical purposes three decades behind. Many organizations lack good governance, financial management, and communications and media skills. Those CSOs that lack strategic vision have spread their resources too thin, providing a wide range of services to communities from educational to social welfare that lack the requisite quality and efficiency.

One of the most common obstacles cited by community organizers is the difficulty in mobilizing diverse groups that constitute the moderate majority. Unlike extremist groups that have developed cohesive platforms and streamlined talking points (despite their ideological differences), moderate groups remain fragmented. Consensus building amongst moderates can prove difficult, and their efforts are frequently stalled due to internal disputes. The breakdown of the Sunni Ittihad Council (discussed on page 26) underscores this challenge. Throughout the country, there is also a lack of collaboration between faith-based and non-faith-based networks. As a result, resources are not well-coordinated between organizations pursuing similar objectives.

While Pakistan's civil society has led several initiatives to educate the population about the threat of extremism, public awareness campaigns are conducted on an ad-hoc basis and their content is reactionary (denouncing violence after the fact, rather than pro-actively promoting peace). Following a terrorist attack, there is often a surge of activity among CSOs, however to be more effective, public awareness campaigns should be conducted on a larger scale and with greater frequency, even when there is a lull in violence.

Furthermore, activists in Pakistan face constant security threats particularly in conflict zones and their peripheries. Pakistan has become one of the most dangerous countries for journalists,[117] and as discussed above, moderate scholars are regularly targeted for speaking out against the Taliban. As such, many CSOs are not able to create bold campaigns or address the issue of extremism directly. Instead, moderate religious scholars often imbed their counter-radicalization messages within speeches or events focusing on broader issues.

---

[117] Amin Ahmed, "UNESCO Ranks Pakistan Second Most Dangerous for Journalists," *Dawn,* May 3, 2012, http://dawn.com/2012/05/03/unesco-ranks-pakistan-second-most-dangerous-for-journalists/

Furthermore, in parts of Khyber Pakhtunkhwa and Baluchistan provinces where social development indicators are among the lowest in Pakistan, the institutional capacity of civil society is underdeveloped compared to regions like southern Punjab, hindering community mobilization and project implementation. Insecurity in these regions further limits the activities of moderate groups. In FATA, for example, many moderate faith-based networks have been entirely dismantled.

Finally, as the socio-political climate in Pakistan becomes increasingly defined by Anti-Americanism, moderates are finding it progressively difficult to engage in counter-terrorism activities. There is a perception amongst many Pakistanis that CVE programs are conducted only at the behest of the US as part of a broader Western agenda to interfere in Pakistan's affairs. Increased public awareness campaigns about the urgency of the threat of extremism and the risk it poses for Pakistanis may enable additional CSOs – and the Pakistani society at-large – to take ownership of the CVE agenda.

RECOMMENDATIONS

This section offers recommendations - based on input from civil society leaders and observations from our fieldwork - for strengthening Pakistan's civil society to improve, expand, and replicate peace-building efforts.

1. Rebuild US-Pakistan Relations at the Track II & Track III Levels

Despite the rollercoaster relationship between the US and Pakistan at the military and diplomatic levels, there is still an opportunity to rebuild relations by pursuing a multi-track policy (engaging Pakistani American CSOs at the Track II level, as well as the broader Pakistani diaspora community at the Track III level). Even after US forces withdraw from Afghanistan, Pakistan will remain a geo-strategic interest to the US given its nuclear weapons capability, proximity to Iran, and economic links with China and Saudi Arabia. Disengaging or even reducing civilian assistance to Pakistan at this critical juncture will only further destabilize the country and impair regional security.

The US can strengthen Pakistan's internal capacity to counter extremism by supporting the expansion of counter-terrorism and de-radicalization initiatives, training the next generation of peace-builders, and establishing partnerships with CSOs to administer humanitarian aid and post-conflict reconstruction. Despite widespread criticism of US foreign policy in Pakistan, throughout our research, civil society leaders – both faith-based and secular - expressed a willingness to engage with the US on these issues. This can be accomplished not only through the US government, but also by engaging the Pakistani American community, and harnessing the American business and non-profit sectors to invest in such programming for Pakistan.

In pursuing this approach, the US government should make a distinction between its public diplomacy goals and its national security interests in reducing international terrorism. In the current political climate, these two objectives may not necessarily be achieved simultaneously. While there are several Pakistan-based CSO's that are capable of conducting effective anti-Taliban initiatives that reduce the threat against the US, these organizations may also be staunch critics of American foreign policy objectives and strategies. Therefore, the US should weigh the costs and benefits of strategic objectives when partnering with such organizations.

2. Develop Relationships with the "Right" Groups

In order to develop sustainable relationships, the US should identify Pakistani CSOs that uphold shared values. Viable partners are those who unconditionally reject terrorism, suicide bombings, and Taliban ideologies. Ideal partners should include groups that actively promote tolerance and social cohesion. In addition, policymakers should be weary of "overnight moderates" or those groups that claim to support peace-building but have had a history of providing ideological or material support for the Taliban.

Civil society organizations that uphold shared values and are engaged in promoting peace and inter-ethnic harmony, countering radical narratives and denouncing extremism at an ideological level, as well as providing humanitarian and development assistance to at-risk communities are good examples of CSO's that should be supported and empowered. Many such organizations have been named in this report.

The US Embassy and consulates, as well as prominent international organizations, can help determine additional potential partners by increasing engagement with Pakistani CSOs. As discussed above, by developing relations with senior community leaders within moderate networks, US policymakers and international development organizations can cultivate relationships with a broad cross-section of Pakistanis.

3. Empower the Next Generation of Pakistani Leaders

Although Pakistani youth activists have the potential to lead counter-extremism programs in Pakistan, they lack the platforms to achieve and utilize their capacity. Youth require civic engagement training so that they can channel their energy in peaceful, productive outlets. Pakistani development organizations such as the Strengthening Participatory Organization (SPO) or the Jinnah Institute could partner with USAID to provide "government 101" training for youth from faith-based and non-faith-based organizations to teach them how to effectively resolve their grievances with local and national public officials.

For Pakistan's next generation to coordinate a countrywide movement against extremism, youth should be provided substantial training in social mobilization, leadership development and non-profit management. In addition, young civil society leaders require strategic development skills to harness the energy of volunteers beyond the immediacy of crisis situations.

To address these challenges, the US government should prioritize CVE program funding for training workshops and seminars within Pakistan. In addition, the US should allocate International Visitor Leadership Program funding for youth exchanges that focus on developing leadership skills. Particular attention should be given to involving youth from lower and lower-middle class communities in these initiatives.

4. Train CSOs to Expand and Improve Upon Existing Programs

In addition to supporting the development of new counter-extremism programming, the US should invest in developing the capacity of CSOs to improve *existing* programs with a proven track record. Relevant US government agencies such as USAID should expand their strategic objectives (e.g. good governance) to focus on developing Pakistan's civil society by offering training programs. Similarly, offices with funding authority such as the US Embassy in Islamabad should allocate a portion of its Countering Violent Extremism (CVE) funding towards training initiatives for peace-building organizations (e.g. conferences, seminars or workshops).

Specific areas that require attention include:

<u>*Non-Profit Management & Capacity Building Training*</u>: Pakistani CSOs can be categorized into two broad groups: those organizations that receive funding and support from international organizations, and those that are indigenous and rely on grassroots community support. The latter often suffer from poor institutional capacity and mismanagement, and lack transparent decision-making processes. In addition, some organizations are dominated by single personalities and lack horizontal leadership development opportunities, which inhibits sustainability. They require leadership and good governance training to strengthen their institution's core capabilities to expand their projects so that they can increase their impact at the local and national levels.

Financial Management Training: In terms of financial transparency, many organizations do not make their records available to the public. In addition, sources of funding and expenditures are not disclosed. They also lack the infrastructure to track the number of volunteers operating within their networks, or the impact of their work. This is a prohibitive challenge for CSOs that are applying to international organizations that require financial or annual reports. Grassroots CSOs in particular require record-keeping and financial management training.

Civic Education Development: Pakistani youth are largely disenfranchised and frustrated with the lack of socio-economic opportunities. While some are anxious to become active in their communities, without productive outlets to channel their energy, many youth engage in destructive and sometimes violent acts of social protest. As part of the US government's democracy promotion agenda, the US can support community organizers in Pakistan to provide civic education and training to youth.

Emergency Management & Humanitarian Relief Distribution Training: Development organizations operating in post-conflict and disaster-affected regions tend to focus on immediate relief rather than sustainable development initiatives. These groups require emergency management and humanitarian relief distribution training to effectively compete against radical charities that have sophisticated distribution mechanisms. In addition, they require skill sets to expand their donor base, improve financial accountability, accelerate distribution of goods and services, strengthen communication with volunteers, and improve their marketing and visibility.

Coalition-Building Assistance: CSOs engaged in peace-building efforts need to collaborate and coordinate resources with other organizations involved in similar efforts. To effectively building partnership and coalitions, CSOs require communications, consensus building, and conflict resolution skills to formulate coherent agendas and prevent internal fissures.

Communications & Media Training: CSOs, particularly traditional Muslim networks, lack communications and media training to disseminate their anti-terror messages to broader audiences. Traditional Muslim scholars, for example, have the capacity to speak at great lengths to promote peace within an orthodox religious paradigm that is palatable to at-risk youth, but lack skills to synthesize their arguments into brief media sound bites. Furthermore, they lack the skills to market their anti-Taliban messaging to non-religious audiences. Public relations firms could help fine-tune their messaging. Similarly, marketing firms could help CSOs disseminate their messages to broader populations.

Social Media Skills Building: In an age where the internet is playing an increasingly menacing role in radicalizing youth, civil society leaders – in particular religious scholars - need to be integrated into modern technological platforms and online social networking sites. With the appropriate training, community leaders can harness the digital age and share de-radicalization seminars and lectures on YouTube and Facebook.

5. Cultivate Relationships with Pakistani Diaspora

With over one-million Pakistanis living in the US, the Pakistani-American diaspora community is one of the largest in the world and has an immense potential to enhance the strength and growth of Pakistan's civil society.[118] Pakistani-Americans with active linkages in Pakistan can work with organizations based in Pakistan to provide institutional capacity training. By increasing the involvement of Pakistani-Americans, the positive experiences of successful diaspora communities can improve public perceptions of the US in

---

[118] "US-EU Expert CVE Meeting on Pakistan and Pakistani Diaspora Communities," Brussels, January 24-25, 2012.

Pakistan. The diaspora can also be a valuable funding mechanism for groups who fear being stigmatized for receiving US government funding. Several leaders mentioned that they would prefer receiving funds from Muslim and/or Pakistani organizations, which would be legitimate to their local constituencies, rather than directly from the US Government. Using these groups as facilitators and program managers is also advantageous to the US because it will provide better fiscal accountability and transparency.

The US government should facilitate new opportunities for the diaspora community to be engaged in Pakistan. For example, the US Government could facilitate exchanges between traditional Muslim networks in Pakistan with Pakistanis in the US who are promoting tolerance and social harmony so that they can explore best practices and avenues for collaboration. The State Department's Pakistan Desk could also host quarterly round-table forums with diaspora communities in major American cities (e.g. Houston, New York, and Washington DC) to foster dialogue and brainstorming on development ideas. In addition, organizations such as the American Pakistan Foundation, which largely focuses on social and economic issues could be expanded to provide institutional capacity building training and to carry out peace-building programs with Pakistan-based CSOs.

6. Support Programs that Create a Public Space for Countering Intolerance

Over the past thirty years, Pakistani society has been affected by radical rhetoric espoused by extremist networks. As a result, moderate community leaders are finding it increasingly difficult to publically address sensitive issues. Moreover, in the current socio-political climate, there are few opportunities for Pakistanis to discuss challenging issues such as developing inter-ethnic and inter/intra-faith harmony. Many fear reprisal from the public, especially from religious figures for challenging intolerant social norms. The failure of the moderate community to condemn the murder of Governor Salman Taseer is emblematic of this.

To address this challenge, relevant government-funded programs from the United States Institute of Peace to the United State Commission on International Religious Freedom can work with public intellectuals, religious scholars, and celebrities to develop projects that promote religious freedom and inter-ethnic social harmony, as well as initiatives that denounce sectarian and communal violence. These initiatives should promote religious freedom within an indigenous framework, tapping on historical examples and a lexicon that resonates with the population. In order for these initiatives to succeed, they must be perceived as something germane to Pakistanis and not as part of a Western/American agenda.

Furthermore, it is essential to engage youth on this issue. The State Department's Bureau of Democracy, Human Rights and Labor should support educational programs and debates that engage both university and madrasa students, which spur intellectual discussions on these key issues. In addition, student dialogues and exchanges between disparate ethnic, faith, and ideological groups can help build tolerance and dispel stereotypes that have divided communities and fueled violent extremism.

7. Develop an Integrated "Whole of Civil Society" Approach

Although CSOs are engaged in promoting peace and social harmony, their efforts remain fragmented. The tension that exists between faith-based organizations and secular organizations in Pakistan is commonly viewed as one of the major internal factors that have adversely affected the development of the nonprofit sector in Pakistan.[119] Although they often provide similar services and pursue comparable objectives, they frame their work in different terms. For example, faith-based organizations may appeal to their community for donations according to the Islamic precepts of *zakat* and *sadaqa* (charity), while secular organizations may frame their appeals in terms of promoting fundamental human rights.

Building a nexus between faith-based and non-faith-based organizations will increase synergy and coordination of resources within Pakistan to challenge extremism.[120] Both sectors would certainly benefit from a partnership. Faith-based groups have grassroots capabilities and legitimacy whereas non-faith based organizations tend to have better institutional capacity.

To date, poor communication between these sectors has hindered opportunities to develop a coordinated national anti-extremism strategy. International pressure may be the necessary impetus to bring these groups together. The US government, particularly the US Embassy in Islamabad, should create venues and networking opportunities for these two groups to collaborate and determine best practices for countering violent extremism.

---

[119] Muhammad Asif Iqbal, Hina Khan, Surkhab Javed. "Nonprofit sector in Pakistan: Historical Background." *Social Policy and Development Centre*. 2004, page 38.
[120] Qamar ul Huda, *Crescent and Dove: Peace and Conflict Resolution in Islam*. USIP. 2010, page 222.

CONCLUSION

The deterioration of US-Pakistan relations in the past two years and the persistence of violent extremism in Pakistan indicate that a major paradigm shift is required in US engagement with Pakistan. Ultimately, a strategic partnership with Pakistan's civil society can both rebuild trust at this critical juncture, and usher in a new, more sustainable chapter in US-Pakistan relations.

The desire of Pakistanis to eliminate violent extremism is visible throughout the country. Despite frequent terrorist attacks, civil society organizations across Pakistan have demonstrated their will and capacity to counter Talibanization by devising indigenous mechanisms of countering extremism within a vernacular that appeals to local populations. Our research indicates that Pakistan's civil society is active on five major levels. First, public intellectuals and community leaders promote peace and social cohesion in an indigenous framework that resonates with Pakistanis in urban and rural areas. Second, advocacy groups educate the public about the threat of extremism by publishing pamphlets and organizing public awareness campaigns and rallies. Third, cultural associations and faith-based organizations challenge the validity of the use of violence by denouncing attacks on innocent civilians. Fourth, faith-based organizations detract the credibility of militant groups by challenging them at an ideological level. Finally, community-based organizations deter impoverished communities from turning to charities associated with extremists by providing alternative channels for humanitarian assistance.

Through capacity-building, technical assistance, and material support, the US can help Pakistanis counter extremism in their communities. This strategy will require the US to shift beyond a transactional relationship with civilian and military officials, to one that invests in developing Pakistan's civil society. This does not mean that the US should abandon its current relationships that have been developed at the Track I level; rather, the US should complement these relationships and maximize our leverage with the GoP by investing in developing relations at the Track II and Track III levels as well.

www.ingramcontent.com/pod-product-compliance
Lightning Source LLC
Chambersburg PA
CBHW051354070526
44584CB00025B/3763